WORLD
HISTORY SERIES

The Declaration
of Independence

Titles in the World History Series

WORLD HISTORY SERIES

The Declaration of Independence

by
Don Nardo

LUCENT
BOOKS ®

THOMSON
────★────
GALE

San Diego • Detroit • New York • San Francisco • Cleveland • New Haven, Conn. • Waterville, Maine • London • Munich

THOMSON
━━━━━✦━━━━━
GALE

© 2004 by Lucent Books. Lucent Books is an imprint of The Gale Group, Inc.,
a division of Thomson Learning, Inc.

Lucent Books® and Thomson Learning™ are trademarks used herein under license.

For more information, contact
Lucent Books
27500 Drake Rd.
Farmington Hills, MI 48331-3535
Or you can visit our Internet site at http://www.gale.com

LIBRARY OF CONGRESS CATALOGING-IN-PUBLICATION DATA

Nardo, Don, 1947–
   The Declaration of Independence / by Don Nardo.
     p. cm. — (World history series)
Summary: Discusses the United States Declaration of Independence, covering such
aspects as the decision to separate from Great Britain, the writing of the Declaration,
and the enduring legacy of this document.
Includes bibliographical references and index.
    ISBN 1-59018-293-6 (hardback: alk. paper)
1. United States. Declaration of Independence—Juvenile literature. 2. United States
—Politics and government—1775–1783—Juvenile literature. [1. United States.
Declaration of Independence. 2. United States—Politics and government—1775–1783.]
I. Title.
II. Series.
   E221.N248 2004
   973.3'13—dc21

                         2003010072

Printed in the United States of America

Contents

Foreword

Each year on the first day of school, nearly every history teacher faces the task of explaining why his or her students should study history. One logical answer to this question is that exploring what happened in our past explains how the things we often take for granted—our customs, ideas, and institutions—came to be. As statesman and historian Winston Churchill put it, "Every nation or group of nations has its own tale to tell. Knowledge of the trials and struggles is necessary to all who would comprehend the problems, perils, challenges, and opportunities which confront us today." Thus, a study of history puts modern ideas and institutions in perspective. For example, though the founders of the United States were talented and creative thinkers, they clearly did not invent the concept of democracy. Instead, they adapted some democratic ideas that had originated in ancient Greece and with which the Romans, the British, and others had experimented. An exploration of these cultures, then, reveals their very real connection to us through institutions that continue to shape our daily lives.

Another reason often given for studying history is the idea that lessons exist in the past from which contemporary societies can benefit and learn. This idea, although controversial, has always been an intriguing one for historians. Those who agree that society can benefit from the past often quote philosopher George Santayana's famous statement, "Those who cannot remember the past are condemned to repeat it." Historians who subscribe to Santayana's philosophy believe that, for example, studying the events that led up to the major world wars or other significant historical events would allow society to chart a different and more favorable course in the future.

Just as difficult as convincing students of the importance of studying history is the search for useful and interesting supplementary materials that present historical events in a context that can be easily understood. The volumes in Lucent Books' World History Series attempt to present a broad, balanced, and penetrating view of the march of history. Ancient Egypt's important wars and rulers, for example, are presented against the rich and colorful backdrop of Egyptian religious, social, and cultural developments. The series engages the reader by enhancing historical events with these cultural contexts. For example, in *Ancient Greece,* the text covers the role of women in that society. Slavery is discussed in *The Roman Empire,* as well as how slaves earned their freedom. The numerous and varied aspects of everyday life in these and other societies are explored in each volume of the series. Additionally, the series covers the major political, cultural, and philosophical ideas as the torch of civilization is passed from ancient Mesopotamia and Egypt, through Greece, Rome, Medieval Europe, and other world cultures, to the modern day.

The material in the series is formatted in a thorough, precise, and organized manner. Each volume offers the reader a comprehensive and clearly written overview of an important historical event or period. The topic under discussion is placed in a broad, historical context. For example, *The Italian Renaissance* begins with a discussion of the High Middle Ages and the loss of central control that allowed certain Italian cities to develop artistically. The book ends by looking forward to the Reformation and interpreting the societal changes that grew out of the Renaissance. Thus, students are not only involved in an historical era, but also enveloped by the events leading up to that era and the events following it.

One important and unique feature in the World History Series is the primary and secondary source quotations that richly supplement each volume. These quotes are useful in a number of ways. First, they allow students access to sources they would not normally be exposed to because of the difficulty and obscurity of the original source. The quotations range from interesting anecdotes to farsighted cultural perspectives and are drawn from historical witnesses both past and present. Second, the quotes demonstrate how and where historians themselves derive their information on the past as they strive to reach a consensus on historical events. Lastly, all of the quotes are footnoted, familiarizing students with the citation process and allowing them to verify quotes and/or look up the original source if the quote piques their interest.

Finally, the books in the World History Series provide a detailed launching point for further research. Each book contains a bibliography specifically geared toward student research. A second, annotated bibliography introduces students to all the sources the author consulted when compiling the book. A chronology of important dates gives students an overview, at a glance, of the topic covered. Where applicable, a glossary of terms is included.

In short, the series is designed not only to acquaint readers with the basics of history, but also to make them aware that their lives are a part of an ongoing human saga. Perhaps then they will come to the same realization as famed historian Arnold Toynbee. In his monumental work, *A Study of History*, he wrote about becoming aware of history flowing through him in a mighty current, and of his own life "welling like a wave in the flow of this vast tide."

IMPORTANT DATES IN THE HISTORY OF THE DECLARATION OF INDEPENDENCE

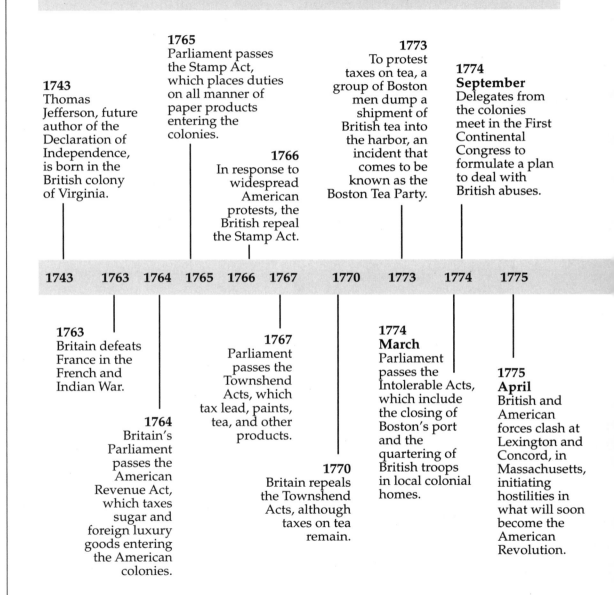

1743
Thomas Jefferson, future author of the Declaration of Independence, is born in the British colony of Virginia.

1765
Parliament passes the Stamp Act, which places duties on all manner of paper products entering the colonies.

1766
In response to widespread American protests, the British repeal the Stamp Act.

1773
To protest taxes on tea, a group of Boston men dump a shipment of British tea into the harbor, an incident that comes to be known as the Boston Tea Party.

1774
September
Delegates from the colonies meet in the First Continental Congress to formulate a plan to deal with British abuses.

1743 | 1763 | 1764 | 1765 | 1766 | 1767 | 1770 | 1773 | 1774 | 1775

1763
Britain defeats France in the French and Indian War.

1764
Britain's Parliament passes the American Revenue Act, which taxes sugar and foreign luxury goods entering the American colonies.

1767
Parliament passes the Townshend Acts, which tax lead, paints, tea, and other products.

1770
Britain repeals the Townshend Acts, although taxes on tea remain.

1774
March
Parliament passes the Intolerable Acts, which include the closing of Boston's port and the quartering of British troops in local colonial homes.

1775
April
British and American forces clash at Lexington and Concord, in Massachusetts, initiating hostilities in what will soon become the American Revolution.

1775
July
The colonists send King George the Olive Branch Petition, a plea for him to restrain Parliament in its ill treatment of the colonies.

1776
June
As a member of a special committee appointed by Congress, Thomas Jefferson writes the rough draft of the Declaration of Independence.

1776
December
George Washington crosses the Delaware River and wins a victory over Britain's German mercenaries.

1775
November
King George declares the colonies to be in open rebellion.

1776
July
Congress debates, amends, and ratifies the Declaration.

1777
Britain's General George Burgoyne tries to invade New York and New England but fails and surrenders to the Americans.

| 1775 | Jan 1776 | Jul 1776 | Dec 1776 | 1777 | 1781 | 1783 |

1776
January
Patriot Thomas Paine publishes *Common Sense*, a pamphlet that bluntly makes the case for American independence.

1776
August
The Declaration's formal signing ceremony takes place (although not all of the congressional delegates sign at this time); the Americans suffer a defeat at the Battle of Long Island.

1781
After the siege of Yorktown, on the Virginia coast, Lord Charles Cornwallis surrenders to Washington, ending the war. The former colonies have won the independence they had declared five years earlier in the Declaration.

1776
June
The Virginia legislature passes a resolution endorsing independence.

1783
Treaty of paris signed.

The Man Who Wrote the Declaration

On February 22, 1861, shortly after taking office as the sixteenth president of the United States, Abraham Lincoln delivered a speech at Independence Hall, in Philadelphia. He stated in part:

> I have never had a feeling politically that did not spring from the sentiments embodied in the Declaration of Independence. I have often pondered over the toils that were endured by the officers and soldiers of the army, who achieved that independence. I have often inquired of myself what great principle or idea it was that kept this confederacy [group of states] so long together.[1]

For a man of such keen intelligence and integrity to express so great a debt to a particular political document speaks highly of that document and its author. Indeed, Lincoln held the man who wrote the Declaration of Independence, Thomas Jefferson, in high esteem.

Lincoln knew that the Revolution that had given birth to the United States had been a collaborative effort. It had required the "toils" not only of "officers and soldiers," but also of legislators, shopkeepers, farmers, and countless oth-ers. Yet the "great principle or idea" behind the Revolution had been stated in a few timeless passages by one man. In the document that had announced American independence to the world, Jefferson had managed to capture the very essence of human longings for freedom, just treatment, and self-government. In so doing, he had enshrined himself as a heroic, almost revered figure for future generations. This was certainly part of the way that Lincoln saw Jefferson—as more than a mere man, as an icon, as perhaps the quintessential American. (Ironically, later ages would come to view Lincoln himself in a similar manner.)

A YOUNG MAN FROM VIRGINIA

Yet Lincoln's more realistic side recognized that the creator of the Declaration was as human as the other American colonists of his era. Jefferson had been only one of hundreds of colonial legislators trying to deal with the mounting abuses of the colonies by the British government. Still, if another of these men had been assigned the task of writing the Declaration, a decidedly different document would have emerged, perhaps one considerably less universal in its sentiments and less memorable.

What kind of person *was* Jefferson, then? What were the special circumstances that shaped his worldview and endowed him with the ability to state the basic truths of the human spirit in a few stirring words and phrases? As Lincoln seemed to imply, any study of the Declaration of Independence must first consider the unique man who wrote it and who became an inspirational figure to later generations of people not only in the United States, but around the world.

Jefferson was born in 1743 at Shadwell, a thousand-acre plantation in the backcountry of the British colony of Virginia. As a boy, he had a close bond with his father, Peter Jefferson, a former surveyor.

Although he lost his father at an early age, Thomas Jefferson found mentors who taught him about politics and law.

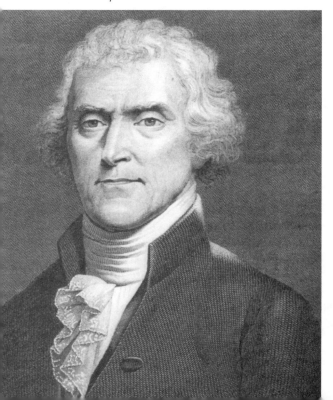

The sudden loss of his paternal mentor in 1757, when Thomas was only fourteen, left the young man vulnerable to a life of aimlessness and sloth. "Thrown on a wide world," Jefferson later remembered,

> among entire strangers, without a friend or guardian to advise, so young, too, and with so little experience of mankind, your dangers great, and still, your safety must rest on yourself. . . . When I recollect that at fourteen years of age the whole care and direction of myself was thrown on myself entirely . . . I am astonished that I did not . . . [become] worthless to society.[2]

Far from becoming worthless to society, Jefferson ended up as one of its most illustrious members. This was partly because he did manage to find more than one "friend or guardian to advise" him. Dr. William Small, a college professor, along with a prominent lawyer, George Wythe, and legislator and fiery orator Patrick Henry befriended the young Jefferson. They showed him how society and politics functioned. They also introduced him to the ideas of John Locke and other European philosophers who advocated basic human rights and freedoms.

"A RAMBLING, VACANT LOOK"

Other colonial leaders were as steeped as Jefferson was in social, political, and philosophical concepts. Yet it was he alone who gave special and unique voice to these ideas in the immortal Declaration. Perhaps one factor that set Jefferson apart from his fellows and allowed him to see the same things they saw in a somewhat different light was that, to some degree at least, he existed in his own private little world. Indeed, as noted scholar Garry Wills points out:

> Jefferson would always be quietly at odds with his surroundings, softly angular, not fitting in. His very bearing suggested this. . . . He had a loose and awkward way of moving. His diffident, abstracted manner was easily mistaken for haughtiness [arrogance].[3]

Patrick Henry, seen here delivering an impassioned speech, introduced Jefferson to the ideas of European philosophers who championed basic human rights.

This odd manner, reminiscent of the universal image of a socially awkward genius, was recorded for posterity by one of Jefferson's contemporaries, William Maclay, in this priceless diary entry:

> Jefferson is a slender man, [and] has rather the air of stiffness in his manner. His clothes seem too small for him. He sits in a lounging manner, on one hip commonly, and with one of his shoulders elevated much above the other. . . . He had a rambling, vacant look, and nothing of that firm, collected deportment [bearing] which I expected [of a noted statesman]. . . .
>
> He spoke almost without ceasing. But even his discourse partook of his personal demeanor. It was loose and rambling, and yet he scattered information wherever he went, and some even brilliant sentiments sparkled from him.[4]

THE RIGHT MAN AT THE RIGHT TIME

Fortunately, Jefferson left behind a mountain of his own writings, many of which give some indication of what went on behind that "rambling, vacant look." They reveal an enormous intellect that was in some ways a product of its time and in others far ahead of it. They also show a man with a tremendous ability to absorb diverse concepts and facts, to organize them, to distill their core meanings, and to express these meanings in simple, inspiring words. These were certainly the special skills and abilities he brought to writing the Declaration of Independence.

In the final analysis, then, as patriot, crusader for human rights, and author of the Declaration, Jefferson emerges much as Lincoln saw him. It is an image of an ordinary man who, by a combination of his unique personal talents and the peculiar circumstances of his life, became *extra*ordinary. He was exactly the right person in the right place and time to create a document that would touch all people in all places and times. His initial intent was merely to explain to the world why the American patriots had decided to split with the mother country. Yet his words and sentiments about human rights and dignity were so universal and so beautifully stated that they later inspired freedom-loving people in numerous countries across the globe; and they will likely continue to do so for a long time to come. As Lincoln put it in an 1859 letter:

> All honor to Jefferson—to the man who, in the concrete pressure of a struggle for national independence by a single people, had the coolness, forecast, and capacity to introduce into a mere revolutionary document an abstract truth, and so to embalm it there, that today and in all coming days, it shall be a rebuke and a stumbling block to the very harbingers [bringers] of . . . tyranny and oppression.[5]

Chapter

1 Britain's Abuses of Its American Colonies

The writing of the Declaration of Independence and the war that followed it between Britain and its American colonies were not sudden, spontaneous events. They were instead actions of last resort, the reluctant reactions of the colonists to what they saw as a long series of abuses by the mother country. The prevailing view was that these abuses had begun many years before Congress ratified the Declaration on July 4, 1776. Over time they had become increasingly insulting and outrageous; moreover, the emotions and differing opinions generated by these events steadily caused the colonists to split into opposing groups. By the time that Thomas Jefferson took up pen to write the Declaration, the population of the colonies was roughly divided into three groups. One consisted of those colonists who desired to remain British subjects no matter what the mother country did; they were known as Loyalists. The second group, the patriots, believed that it would be best for the colonies to split with Britain. The third group, according to patriot leader John Adams, was made up of apathetic people who did not care who ruled them.

The patriots were louder and more active than the members of the other two groups and steadily led the colonies toward a confrontation with Britain. Yet the patriots themselves were often divided

about what course to take. The more radical ones, like Patrick Henry and Samuel Adams, thought fighting was the only way. But others, Jefferson and George Washington among them, hoped for some kind of reconciliation with the British. In the view of these moderates, there might still be a way to patch up the differences between the colonies and mother country.

THE LAND OF OPPORTUNITY

These moderate colonists looked back fondly at the "good old days," so to speak, between Britain and its American colonies. Indeed, they noted, before the mid-1760s, few Americans had had any reason to complain about the way Britain and its chief legislature, Parliament, treated them.

Only a few generations had passed since English settlers had established their first permanent outpost in North America—at Jamestown (in Virginia), in 1607. Other groups of settlers had quickly followed. The Pilgrims landed at Plymouth, in Massachusetts, in 1620; then came the founding of New Hampshire (1623), New York (1624), Connecticut (1633), Maryland (1634), and seven more colonies. The last of the thirteen British colonies, Georgia, was established in

1733, only ten years before Thomas Jefferson was born.

A few of the British subjects who ended up in these colonies came to America to escape religious intolerance in Europe. Yet at the time, none of them thought about giving up their British citizenship, for many of the benefits of that citizenship were widely coveted. The peoples of France, Germany, Spain, and other European powers were still subject largely to the whims of hereditary royalty and had few, if any, civil rights. In contrast, though Britain was not yet a true democracy, the king no longer had the authority to pass laws and impose taxes; Parliament wielded these powers, which meant that the national legislature overshadowed the monarchy. An Englishman could "count on trial by jury if accused of a crime," New York University historian Irwin Unger points out.

> Moreover, he was accorded equal protection under the law; there was not one law for lord and one for commoner, as elsewhere. Nor was the average Englishman entirely without power in governing the realm. Even if few could vote, the English constitution recognized the representative principle that the lawmakers derived their powers, if only indirectly, from those who were expected to obey the laws they imposed.[6]

Patrick Henry (center), like other radical patriots, openly opposed British rule.

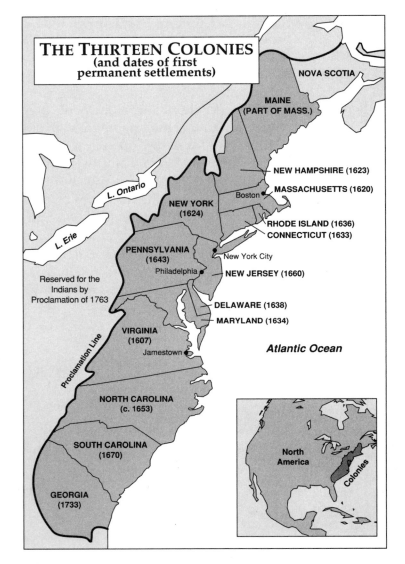

THE THIRTEEN COLONIES
(and dates of first permanent settlements)

NOVA SCOTIA

MAINE (PART OF MASS.)

NEW HAMPSHIRE (1623)

MASSACHUSETTS (1620)
Boston

L. Ontario

NEW YORK (1624)

RHODE ISLAND (1636)
CONNECTICUT (1633)

L. Erie

PENNSYLVANIA (1643)
Philadelphia

New York City

NEW JERSEY (1660)

Reserved for the Indians by Proclamation of 1763

DELAWARE (1638)
MARYLAND (1634)

Proclamation Line

VIRGINIA (1607)
Jamestown

Atlantic Ocean

NORTH CAROLINA (c. 1653)

SOUTH CAROLINA (1670)

North America

Colonies

GEORGIA (1733)

Capitalists could make profits from land speculation, trade, and agriculture, and rulers could enrich their realms. The expectations of Europeans who had only their lives to invest were more modest, perhaps, but ultimately also largely material. They came to acquire the independence that the social and economic systems of England and Europe denied ordinary farmers and laborers. Opportunity was America's basic promise at the beginning and would remain its promise throughout history.[7]

A PEOPLE DOUBLY BLESSED?

Thus, the earliest inhabitants of the thirteen American colonies thought of themselves not as Americans, but as British citizens who lived in America. In their search for better economic and/or religious opportunities and conditions, they had to work hard and take many risks. So they naturally sought to maintain whatever social and psychological stability they could by falling back on their cultural roots. In other words, they brought with them to North America the familiar and comforting political institutions and social customs of the mother country. Eventually, each colony set up its own legisla-

If the minority of colonists who went to America for religious reasons were content to remain British, the vast majority, who had other motives for the trip, certainly felt no different. Of these varied motives, the chief one was economic. As Unger puts it:

The strongest lure of America for Europeans was material opportunity.

ture, for example. And these local political bodies used Britain's Parliament as their model. The British government appointed a governor for each colony. However, in the early 1700s, the colonial legislatures won the right to handle their own local finances, to run their own religious and educational affairs, and to debate freely, even if the royal governor disliked the topic.

As late as the early 1760s, therefore, the vast majority of American colonists felt that they were doubly blessed. On the one hand, they enjoyed the considerable liberal rights of British citizenship. On the other hand, they had economic opportunities that most ordinary citizens back in Britain lacked. True, during the late 1600s and early 1700s, Parliament had enacted a number of trade laws designed to give Britain the lion's share of the benefits of colonial trade. Collectively titled the Navigation Acts, these laws had ensured that all goods would be shipped to England first, regardless of their ultimate destination. As a result, the American colonies had to pay higher prices. Overall, however, the colonies grudgingly accepted such restrictions, partly because they realized that ways could be found to get around most of them.

The Molasses Act, passed by Britain in 1733, was a case in point. It altered direct commerce between the New England colonies and the West Indies by making the ships stop in England along the way. As a countermeasure, the Americans simply smuggled in molasses, which rendered the Molasses Act ineffective. This and similar trade laws had little overall impact on the lives of most Americans. So most colonists, including those who evaded British shipping laws, remained content with British rule and never considered separating from the mother country.

THE OUTRAGE OF 1765

However, that complacent attitude began to change measurably in 1765. This was the year that Parliament passed the Stamp Act, a law that, seen in retrospect, set in motion the string of events that would lead to the Declaration of Independence. The Stamp Act grew out of Britain's dire need for money following its 1763 victory over France in the French and Indian War. As prizes, the British acquired southern Canada and the vast tracts of land lying between the original thirteen colonies and the Mississippi River. These territories needed to be guarded from further French aggression. So British leaders decided it would be prudent to keep large numbers of troops stationed in North America as a precaution.

The problem was that supplying, housing, and paying so many soldiers was hugely expensive. Hoping to shift the burden away from taxpayers in Britain, many members of Parliament thought the best solution was to tax the colonists. First came the American Revenue Act of 1764, which placed taxes on sugar and luxury products, such as wine, silk, and linen, entering the American colonies. Much more burdensome for the colonists was the Stamp Act, passed by Parliament the following year. "It was a heavy tax," historian Samuel E. Morison explains,

bearing on all classes and sections in America. . . . Almost every kind of legal paper . . . appeal or writ of error

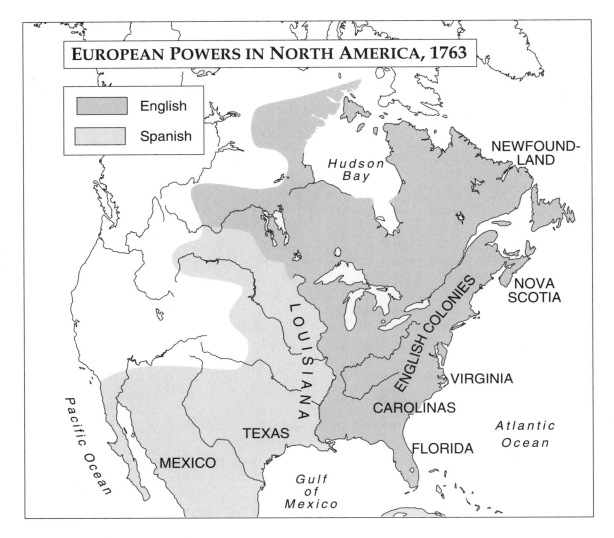

EUROPEAN POWERS IN NORTH AMERICA, 1763

English

Spanish

NEWFOUND-LAND

Hudson Bay

NOVA SCOTIA

ENGLISH COLONIES

L O U I S I A N A

VIRGINIA

CAROLINAS

Atlantic Ocean

TEXAS

FLORIDA

Pacific Ocean

MEXICO

Gulf of Mexico

. . . school or college degree diploma . . . local licensing fee, a lawyer's license to practice . . . land warrant or deed . . . [copy] of a newspaper . . . copy of an almanac . . . [and even] playing cards . . . had to be engrossed or printed on specially stamped paper sold by the official distributors, or brought to a stamp office to be embossed with the stamp and the duty [tax] paid.[8]

It is important to note that some members of Parliament recognized that the new law was unfair, even unjust, and rightly predicted that it would not be well received in the colonies. They balked when one of the backers of the Stamp Act, Charles Townshend, arrogantly asked:

Will these Americans, children planted by our care, nourished up by our indulgence until they are grown to a degree of strength and opulence and protected by our arms, will they grudge to contribute . . . to relieve us from the heavy [financial] burden which we lie under?[9]

At this, an Irish-born veteran of the French and Indian War leaped to his feet and shouted:

> They planted by your care? No! Your oppressions planted 'em in America. They fled your tyranny to a then uncultivated and inhospitable country. . . . They nourished by your indulgence? They grew by your neglect of 'em. . . . [Later you sent] persons to rule over them . . . to spy out their liberty, to misrepresent their actions and to prey upon 'em. . . . They protected by your arms? They have nobly taken up arms in your defense. . . . Remember [that] I this day told you so: that same spirit of freedom which actuated these people at first, will accompany them still.[10]

REACTIONS TO THE STAMP ACT

Despite these reasoned words, which soon proved prophetic, Parliament passed the Stamp Act by a vote of 245 to 49. When this news reached America, many colonial legislators were outraged to say the least. In Virginia's assembly, the House of Burgesses, Patrick Henry loudly argued that Virginians should not have to pay any taxes imposed by non-Virginians. Furthermore, any person who supported such taxes should be viewed as an enemy of the people of Virginia. These defiant words soon appeared in newspapers all over the colonies. Inspired by them, in October 1765 twenty-seven delegates from nine of the thirteen colonies met in New York in what came to be called the "Stamp Act Congress." These men adopted a resolution urging the British to repeal the Stamp Act.

The Stamp Act, a British law that levied a tax on most colonial paper products, met with violent opposition in the colonies.

Meanwhile, reactions on the American street were not nearly so formal and polite. People from all walks of life protested loudly, often resorting to violence. According to Morison:

> In every continental seaport there formed a group of middle-class citizens who called themselves "Sons of Liberty." . . . These liberty boys, often disguising themselves as workmen or sailors, coerced [stamp] distributors into resigning, burned the stamp paper, and incited people to attack unpopular local characters. On the very day (November 1, 1765) that the Stamp Act came into operation, a howling New York mob . . . forced [the lieutenant governor] to take refuge on board a British warship. It then . . . broke into the governor's coach house, destroyed his carriages, and forced the officer in charge of the stamped paper to burn it. . . . In Boston, the stamp distributor was hanged in effigy and his shop pulled down, after which the mob turned its attention to the royal customs collectors. . . . It gutted their houses, burned their furniture, and tossed their books and papers into the street.[11]

The net effect of all these formal and informal protests was to nullify the Stamp Act. Parliament saw no choice but to repeal it and did so in March 1766. Thrilled, American colonists celebrated joyfully and even the most vehement former protesters reaffirmed their loyalty to the mother country. To them, the repeal appeared to confirm that British leaders had learned their lesson and would henceforth treat the colonies with respect and justice.

THE TROUBLE WITH TEA

It soon became clear, however, that British leaders had *not* learned this lesson. They still needed money to pay for the upkeep of their troops stationed in North America and searched for some way to secure the funds. In 1767 Charles Townshend, who had viewed the American protests against the Stamp Act as outrageous, proposed a new revenue scheme. It consisted of a series of import duties on goods Britain shipped to the colonies, including lead, glass, paints, paper, and tea. Townshend was careful this time to point out that the tax was "external"; that is, it was collected before the goods left colonial docks, in contrast to the stamp tax, which people had to pay "internally," when they were buying goods in shops.

A number of people on both sides of the Atlantic were not fooled into thinking that this distinction between external and internal taxes mattered very much. To combat the Townshend duties, many American merchants boycotted the British goods in question. At the same time, colonial leaders on all levels encouraged people to make glass, paint, and some other products locally, to wear American-made clothes, and to drink only tea that had been grown in America. Overall, this approach was successful. The volume of imports from Britain diminished by almost a third, which forced Parliament to repeal the Townshend duties fewer than three years after they had been enacted.

There was an exception, however, namely, the tax on imported tea, which eventually led to more trouble. The period from 1771 to 1773 remained relatively quiet in the colonies, as most Americans seemed happy enough that the rest of the Townshend duties were gone. In contrast, the more militant Sons of Liberty, a secret group dedicated to fighting for civil liberties, kept trying to convince people to rise up and protest the remaining tea duty. Their effort probably would have come to nothing had the British government not committed another serious blunder, one destined to put the colonies back on the path toward independence. "The occasion for this misstep," Unger explains,

> was the distress of the British East India Company. After decades of growing profit in trade with India and the Far East, the company had been brought to the edge of ruin by mis-

management and fraud. Its remaining asset, eighteen million pounds of tea, could not be sold because taxes in Britain and America made smuggled Dutch tea cheaper. To help the company, the British government, under the Tea Act, agreed to allow it to sell its tea in the colonies under its own agents. By eliminating American middlemen, the company might pay the . . . tax and still undersell smuggled tea. . . . The Tea Act offended Americans. . . . In the eyes of many colonial merchants, [it] suggested that Britain might use its power to regulate imperial commerce by conferring special privileges on cooperative colonial businessmen while denying them to unfriendly ones.[12]

Incensed by what they saw as a new threat to their liberty, American merchants,

A British Politician Calls for Repealing the Stamp Act

Among the American supporters in Britain's Parliament was William Pitt, earl of Chatham. In January 1766, he spoke the following words (quoted in Richard B. Morris's The American Revolution, 1763–1783: A Bicentennial Collection*), urging his colleagues to repeal the Stamp Act.*

"The Commons of America, represented by their several assemblies, have ever been in the possession of the exercise of this, their constitutional right, of giving and granting their own money. They would have been slaves if they had not enjoyed it. At the same time, this kingdom . . . has always bound the colonies by her laws, by her regulations, and restrictions in trade, in navigation, in manufactures, in everything, except that of taking their money out of their pockets without their consent."

"We Cannot Be Happy Without Being Free"

Late in 1767, a Philadelphia lawyer named John Dickinson began publishing his twelve Farmer's Letters *in which he stated that the Townshend Acts were just another unfair British revenue scheme. The following excerpt is from the twelfth letter (quoted in Samuel E. Morison's* Sources and Documents Illustrating the American Revolution*).*

"Let these truths be indelibly impressed on our minds—that we cannot be happy without being free—that we cannot be free without being secure in our property—that we cannot be secure in our property if without our consent others may . . . take it away—that taxes imposed on us by Parliament do thus take it away—that duties raised for the sole purpose of raising money are taxes—that attempts to lay such duties should be instantly and firmly opposed—that this opposition can never be effectual unless it is the united effort of these provinces."

craftsmen, and others, including radical elements like the Sons of Liberty, condemned the Tea Act. In three of the four major colonial ports where tea shipments arrived—New York, Philadelphia, and Charleston—protesters stopped the ships from docking. In Boston leading patriots demanded that the colonial governor do the same. But he refused. In retaliation, on December 16, 1773, a gang of local men, most of them members of the Sons of Liberty, disguised themselves as Indians and black slaves and converged on Boston's docks. While a huge crowd of locals watched, the men divided into groups and boarded the three ships carrying the imported tea. Next, they persuaded the customs officers guarding the tea that the safest thing they could do was go ashore and stay out of the way. Finally, the mock Indians and slaves dumped all 342 chests of tea into the harbor.

Reactions to the Tea Party

Although no one was physically hurt in the incident, it created an uproar. Patriot and future U.S. president John Adams immediately saw it as a crucial turning point. "This is the most magnificent movement of all!" he scratched in his diary.

> There is a dignity, a majesty, a sublimity, in this last effort of the patriots that I greatly admire. The people should never rise without doing something to be remembered, something notable and striking. This destruction of the tea is so bold, so daring, so firm, intrepid, and inflexible, and it must have so important consequences, and so lasting, that I can't but consider it as an epocha [dawning of a new era] in history![13]

In Britain, by contrast, King George, most members of Parliament, and a majority of the citizenry viewed the so-called Boston Tea Party as willful destruction of property and the act of an uncivilized mob. In Parliament a number of members started talking tough about retaliation. One of the few American supporters in the legislature, William Pitt, warned that it would be rash and unfair to punish all the people of Massachusetts or Boston for the acts of a few radicals. It would also almost certainly inflame passions in all of the colonies. But his cautionary words were met with derision. One hardliner exclaimed, "'Tis said America will be exasperated" by the punishment Parliament will mete out. "Will she then take arms? She has neither army, navy, money, nor men."[14]

This conceited, inflexible attitude prevailed. Between March and June 1774, Parliament enacted its retribution against the offending colonists by passing the Coercive Acts. Their very name indicated that they were designed to coerce the Americans, specifically the Bostonians, into submission. In the colonies, the legislation became known under a different name—the Intolerable Acts. This description was apt. One of them, the Boston Port Act, closed the port of Boston until such time as the colonists paid for the lost tea. Another provision, the Massachusetts

The Boston Tea Party encouraged the American colonies to unite in opposition to British abuses.

Government and Administration of Justice Act, severely restricted the authority of local government. Still another, the Quartering Act, gave the royal governor the power to quarter, or house, British troops in colonial homes. (Before this, the troops had camped out on Boston Common.)

The intended effect of the Coercive Acts was to make Massachusetts an example. Parliament hoped that administering a hard slap on its wrist would eliminate further resistance to British policies in the other colonies. However, this approach completely backfired. All of the American colonies began to unite and oppose what they viewed as the newest barrage of British abuses. A colonial communications network, the "committees of correspondence," which had been organized a few years before, spread the news of Boston's troubles far and wide. And ships from sister colonies ran the Boston blockade and brought in thousands of bushels of corn and wheat and tons of other relief supplies.

Meanwhile, prominent colonial leaders were not idle. Men who had long considered themselves moderates and wanted no trouble with Britain felt they could not remain quiet. On May 17, 1774, eighty-nine members of Virginia's House of Burgesses, including George Washington, Thomas Jefferson, and Patrick Henry, held a secret meeting in the Raleigh Tavern in Williamsburg. (The spontaneous gathering was technically illegal since Virginia's governor had only hours before dissolved the Virginia legislature after its members had stated that the Boston Port Act was a hostile invasion of the colonies.) The Virginians remained at the tavern until they had drafted a resolution.

"We are . . . clearly of [the] opinion," it began,

> that an attack made on one of our sister colonies, to compel submission to arbitrary taxes, is an attack made on all British America, and threatens ruin to the rights of all, unless the united wisdom of the whole be applied. And for this purpose it is recommended to the committee of correspondence, that they communicate, with their several corresponding committees, on the expediency of appointing deputies from the several colonies . . . to meet in general Congress.[15]

A CALL FOR THE KING TO ACT REASONABLY

The "general Congress" called for by the leading Virginians became known as the First Continental Congress. It took place about four months later, in September 1774, in Philadelphia. Twelve of the thirteen colonies sent delegates in hopes of finding a peaceful way of dealing with what they saw as growing threats to American liberty. At this point, few of the delegates even considered the notion of separating from the mother country. Even these few radicals, among them Samuel Adams and Patrick Henry, did not really want such a split. They simply believed that, given the way events were transpiring, it appeared to be inevitable. That these radical patriots did not represent a majority of the population of the colonies is illustrated by the verbal abuse they often received, especially from colonial Loyalists. "I wish they were all scalped," a Massachusetts farmer exclaimed. "Damn the Congress to hell."[16]

The majority of the delegates did not feel they deserved such condemnation, either from local Loyalists or from the British themselves. The moderate patriots felt fully justified in taking exception with the way the mother country had been treating them of late and pointed out that the purpose of the Congress was only to find some way of reconciling with Britain. They desired for British leaders to repeal the Intolerable Acts and give up attempts to tax the colonies. The delegates also wanted Britain to respect the right of the colonists to trade as they pleased and to govern their own internal affairs without interference from an outside power. These were the themes of several pamphlets written by various delegates just prior to the Philadelphia meeting.

In retrospect, the most important of these writings was Jefferson's *Summary View of the Rights of British America*. It contained germs of some of the same ideas he would state later in more sweeping terms in the Declaration of Independence. Britain had no right to dissolve or interfere with colonial legislatures, Jefferson wrote, because it was in "the nature of things" for a people to govern their own affairs. "Your majesty, or your governors," he said,

> have carried [their] power beyond every limit known, or provided for, by the laws. After dissolving one house of representatives, they have refused to call another, so that, for a great length of time, the legislature provided by the laws has been out of existence. From the nature of things, every society must at all times possess

Upset with the terms of the Coercive Acts, the First Continental Congress advised King George III (pictured) to hear their grievances.

> within itself the sovereign powers of legislation. The feelings of human nature revolt against the supposition of a state so situated as that it may not in any emergency provide against dangers which perhaps threaten immediate ruin. While those bodies are in existence to whom the people have delegated the powers of legislation, they alone possess and may exercise those powers.[17]

In the same document, Jefferson daringly called the British king by name and in words bordering on insolence challenged him to act fairly and honestly; it was clearly an indirect, not-so-veiled way of saying that the British had *not* been fair and honest in recent dealings with the colonies.

Kings are the servants, not the proprietors of the people. Open your breast, sire, to liberal and expanded thought. Let not the name of George the third be a blot on the page of history. . . . You have no ministers for American affairs, because you have none taken from among us, nor amenable to the laws on which they are to give you advice. It behooves you, therefore, to think and act for yourself and your people. The great principles of right and wrong are legible to every reader; to pursue them requires not the aid of many counselors. The whole art of government consists in the art of being honest. Only aim to do your duty and mankind will give you credit where you fail.[18]

THE SUFFOLK RESOLVES

The delegates to the First Continental Congress reviewed Jefferson's pamphlet. And many of them agreed with its contents. They did not adopt it or its language, however, as the official statement

---

BRITISH TROOPS SENT TO AMERICA UNLAWFULLY?

In this excerpt from his Summary View of the Rights of British America *(quoted in* Merrill D. Peterson's *Thomas* Jefferson: Writings*), Jefferson complained about the British military presence in the colonies.*

"His majesty has from time to time sent among us large bodies of armed forces, not made up of the people here, nor raised by the authority of our laws. Did his majesty possess such a right as this, it might swallow up all our other rights whenever he should think proper. But his majesty has no right to land a single armed man on our shores, and those whom he sends here are liable to our laws. . . . To render these proceedings still more criminal against our laws, instead of subjecting the military to the civil powers, his majesty has expressly made the civil subordinate to the military. But can his majesty thus put down all law under his feet? Can he erect a power superior to that which erected himself? He has done it indeed by force; but let him remember that force cannot get right."

of their meeting. Instead, they concentrated most of their time and energy on a plan proposed on September 28 by Pennsylvania's Joseph Galloway. Called the Plan of Union, it sought to meet the British halfway, in a sense, by creating an American version of Parliament. This colonial legislature, representing all thirteen colonies, would work with the British Parliament. Each would be given veto powers over the other in political and other matters having to do with the American colonies.

Many of the delegates liked Galloway's plan. However, after hearing about the Suffolk Resolves, they put it aside. These resolutions had been penned by Massachusetts patriot Joseph Warren and passed in early September by a secret meeting of representatives from a number of towns in the Boston area. The resolutions advocated that Massachusetts defy the royal governor and create its own government. They also called for a sweeping economic boycott of British goods and warned the citizenry to begin arming in case it became necessary to fight for their homes.

After some debate, the Continental Congress accepted the Suffolk Resolves. Then, on October 14, the delegates published their own resolves, denouncing the Intolerable Acts and asserting that the British had no right to interfere in colonial affairs without the consent of the colonists themselves. Congress also listed all of the acts passed by the British since 1763 that it thought offensive and illegal and demanded their repeal. However, the delegates still stopped short of calling for a split with the mother country. Hope for eventual reconciliation with the British was still foremost in the thoughts of the majority of American patriots. At this juncture, they had no way of knowing how fast crucial events would move in the days ahead. The reality was that they were rapidly approaching the fateful point of no return, beyond which independence would be the only option.

2 The Decision to Declare Independence

After the passage of more than two centuries, it is difficult to say with confidence exactly which event constituted the point of no return on the road to the Declaration of Independence and the war fought to win that independence. The Boston Tea Party was provocative and created tensions. And the 1774 meeting of the Continental Congress, the Suffolk Resolves, and the language of Jefferson's *Summary View* were all certainly defiant in tone. Yet none of these was serious enough to provoke or justify a war. As late as the opening months of 1775, most of the colonial leaders, including Jefferson himself, were still hoping to patch up their differences with the king and Parliament.

Therefore, the point of no return occurred between early 1775 and mid-1776, when the Declaration itself was issued. In examining the events of this fateful period, one fact stands out in sharp relief. Up until April 1775, no organized warfare had occurred between British soldiers and American militiamen (or "minutemen," mainly farmers and shopkeepers who stood ready to grab their muskets, fight, and then return home). In that month, both American and British blood was shed in open battle. Whatever the real historical point of no return may have been, in the minds of most of the colonists, it was when the British first entered their towns and fired on them. The prevailing contemporary view was aptly expressed by a Philadelphia farmer who joined the American army not long after 1776:

Had we begun this quarrel, had we demanded some new privileges unknown to the [British] Constitution, or some commercial licenses incompatible with the general interests of the empire, had we presumed to legislate for Great Britain, or plotted [to overthrow the monarchy], there would then be some plausible apology for the severest hostile treatment we have received. But what have we done? . . . We asserted our rights and petitioned for justice. Was this a crime? . . . We repeated our petitions for redress; was this a crime? We suffered ourselves to be insulted by the introduction of an armed force to dragoon us into obedience; we suffered them to take possession of our towns and fortifications, still waiting with decent and anxious expectation [for] justice, humanity, and generosity [from Britain]; was this a crime? . . . Nor did we once lift the sword even in our defense, until provoked to it by a wanton commencement of hostilities on their part.[19]

THE THREAT OF VIOLENCE LOOMS

In retrospect, it seems clear that the opening of hostilities in April 1775 was neither inevitable nor a foregone conclusion. British commanders stationed in Boston might have avoided the outbreak of violence had they not been so contemptuous of the patriots' grievances and so heavy-handed in their responses to potential threats. There was no effort by British officers to meet with local patriots in an effort to reduce tensions. Nor did the British try to avoid an armed confrontation by keeping a low profile.

In defense of the British officers, however, it must be pointed out that they believed the threat of a sudden attack by some of the more radical colonists was very real. The British were well aware of how angry most of the locals were over the Intolerable Acts. They also knew that many had followed the advice of the Suffolk Resolves and begun to arm themselves. There was even direct proof that some colonists would not hesitate to use these weapons, as shown in an incident later reported by John Howe, a British officer stationed in Boston. In early April 1775, he was ordered to travel through the countryside in civilian clothes and quietly ascertain the mood of the populace. Approaching the small rural home of an elderly couple, Howe found the man cleaning a gun. According to Howe's later account:

I asked him what he was going to kill, as he was so old, I should not think he could take sight at any game. He said there was a flock of redcoats at Boston, which he expected would be here soon. He meant to try and hit some of

Despite the defiant overtones in Thomas Jefferson's Summary View, *the essay stopped short of advocating a split with Britain.*

A

S U M M A R Y   V I E W

OF THE

R I G H T S

O F

B R I T I S H   A M E R I C A.

SET FORTH IN SOME

R E S O L U T I O N S

INTENDED FOR THE

I N S P E C T I O N

OF THE PRESENT

D E L E G A T E S

OF THE

P E O P L E   O F   V I R G I N I A.

N O W   I N

C O N V E N T I O N.

By a NATIVE, AND MEMBER OF THE HOUSE, OF BURGESSES.
by Thomas Jefferson.

WILLIAMSBURG:
PRINTED BY CLEMENTINA RIND.

them, as he expected they would be very good marks. I asked the old man how he expected to fight. He said, "Open field fighting, or any other way to kill them redcoats!" I asked him how old he was. He said, "Seventy-seven and never was killed yet." I asked the old man if there were any tories [the British name for Loyalists] nigh [near] there. He said there was one tory house in sight, and he wished it was in flames. The old man says, "Old woman, put in the bullet pouch a handful of buckshot, as I understand the English like an assortment of plums!"[20]

The new governor of Massachusetts, General Thomas Gage, was aware of this and other ominous reports about belligerent colonists. Not long after hearing Howe's story about the old couple, Gage received word from another of his undercover operatives that some patriots had collected a large store of weapons in the village of Concord, twenty-one miles west of Boston. Gage worried that these arms would be circulated to local rebels. So during the night of April 18, he quietly assembled about seven hundred British troops and ordered them to proceed to Concord and destroy the weapons.

"DISPERSE, YE REBELS, DISPERSE!"

The redcoats, led by Lieutenant Colonel Francis Smith, marched for several hours in the dark, sure that they had achieved the element of surprise. But they were wrong. The colonists had far more undercover eyes and ears than the British

---

THE REAL REASONS FOR THE WAR?

In 1781, five years after he had written the Declaration of Independence, Thomas Jefferson gave the following highly oversimplified explanation of the causes of the American Revolution (quoted in volume 16 of A.A. Lipscomb and A.E. Bergh's Writings of Thomas Jefferson) *to a Native American chief who was visiting him.*

"You find us, brother, engaged in a war with a powerful nation. Our forefathers were Englishmen, inhabitants of a little island beyond the great water, and, being distressed for land, they came and settled here. As long as we were young and weak, the English . . . made us carry all our wealth to their country, to enrich them; and, not satisfied with this, they at length began to say we . . . should do whatever they ordered us. We were now grown up and felt ourselves strong; we knew we were [as] free as they . . . and we were determined to be free as long as we should exist. For this reason they made war on us."

The battle at Lexington marked the first clash between American militiamen and British regulars.

did, and warnings had sped well ahead of the night marchers. As dawn broke, the British soldiers approached the village of Lexington, not far from Concord, and heard the local church bells ringing out an alarm.

As the redcoats entered the village, they found a force of some eighty armed colonial militiamen waiting for them on the town green. The British second in command, Major John Pitcairn, called out, "Lay down your arms!" Another British officer shouted, "Disperse, ye rebels, disperse!" Captain John Parker, who led the local militiamen, saw that his men were hopelessly outnumbered; and in any case, he did not want to be responsible for starting a war. So he ordered his men to back off and hold their fire. (The often-cited claim that Parker told his men to "stand your ground" and defiantly asserted, "If they mean to have a war, let it begin here," is almost certainly false.) It was too late, however. Suddenly a shot rang out, from which side no one knows to this day. Believing they were under attack, the redcoats opened fire, and in the din of the discharging muskets, they could not hear Pitcairn shouting, "Cease firing!"[21]

At this point, Lieutenant Colonel Smith had the presence of mind to have a drummer beat out the signal for cease-fire. And when the smoke had cleared, eight Americans lay dead on the green. Someone advised Smith that it would be wise to return to Boston, as the incident was bound to arouse more local militiamen. (In fact, at that moment thousands of armed colonists were converging on the area from as far away as Connecticut and New Hampshire.) But Smith, who held the colonists in contempt, arrogantly and unwisely ordered the expedition to continue.

The British troops reached Concord at about 8 A.M. At North Bridge, roughly a mile from the village green, they saw a force of more than four hundred armed militiamen approaching. The American commander, Colonel James Barrett, ordered his men not to fire first. Apparently they followed this order, for the opening shots of the battle came from some panicky young British regulars. After a deadly exchange of musket fire, several redcoats lay dead beside the bridge.

Suddenly, the odds had turned in the Americans' favor. As many as six thousand more militiamen were on their way to reinforce Barrett's ranks. This time, Lieutenant Colonel Smith saw the wisdom of turning tail and heading back to Boston. As his men marched along, many of the militiamen followed and fired at them almost continuously from behind rocks and trees. On finally reaching Boston, Smith's company had casualties numbering 73 dead, 174 wounded, and 26 missing. By contrast, the Americans had lost 50 killed and 34 wounded.

LAST-DITCH ATTEMPTS TO AVOID WAR

The news of the battles at Lexington and Concord rapidly spread through the colonies. All patriots immediately condemned the British for provoking the fighting, while the more radical patriots insisted that there could now be no turn-ing back, no realistic way of stopping the onset of an all-out war for American independence. The most eloquent reaction was that of Thomas Paine, an English essayist who had emigrated to America and joined the patriots in 1774. "By referring the matter from argument to arms," he later wrote,

> a new era for politics has struck—a new method of thinking has arisen. All plans, proposals, etc. prior to the nineteenth of April, *i.e.* to the commencement of hostilities, are like the almanacs of the last year; which though proper then . . . are useless now. . . . The independence of America should have been considered as dating its era from . . . *the first musket that was fired against her.*[22]

However, in spite of the widespread indignation and anger in the colonies over the battles, the moderate patriots still tried to avert full-fledged war and separation from Britain. A second meeting of Congress was held in Philadelphia in May 1775. As a precaution, the delegates set in motion the process that would eventually lead to the formation of an army to defend the colonies. They proclaimed the Massachusetts militiamen who had fought the British the "Army of the United Colonies" and appointed Virginia's George Washington as commander in chief of those troops and any others that might be raised. At the same time, though, Congress issued a document clarifying its position. "We mean not to dissolve that union which has so long and so happily subsisted between us [and Britain]," it stated. "We have not raised armies with ambitious designs of separation from Great Britain, and establishing independent states."[23]

The moderates remained firm in this conciliatory approach even after another, larger battle erupted on June 17, 1775. (About 2,200 British regulars and 3,200 American militiamen clashed at Boston's Breed's Hill, often mistakenly called the Battle of Bunker Hill; the British won the hill, but their losses were so great that the Americans saw it as a strategic victory and major morale booster.) Several weeks later, on July 8, Congress issued the Olive Branch Petition, drafted by moderate patriots John Jay and John Dickinson. A last-ditch effort to avoid all-out war, the petition asked King George to give serious consideration to American grievances concerning the recent "abuses" of Parliament.

The hopes of the moderates were dashed, however, when the king refused to read the petition. Even worse, in early November news reached the colonies that George had declared the colonies to be in a state of open rebellion. "Misled by dangerous and ill-designing men, and forgetting the allegiance which they owe to" the mother country, the proclamation stated, the troublemakers had engaged in "the obstruction of lawful commerce, and to

As they approach the American lines in the Battle of Bunker Hill, waves of British soldiers march over the bodies of their dead comrades.

the oppression of our loyal subjects," and "have at length proceeded to open and avowed rebellion, by arraying themselves in a hostile manner." These traitors, said the king, were "ordering and levying war against us." Furthermore, all those Americans still loyal to Britain were "bound by law to be aiding and assisting in the suppression of such rebellion, and to disclose and make known all traitorous conspiracies and attempts against us, our crown and dignity." The Loyalists should "make known all treasons" and report to the authorities "full information of all persons . . . now in open arms and rebellion against our government."[24]

A RISING SPIRIT OF INDEPENDENCE

The king's callous condemnation of the patriots changed the minds of many moderates in their ranks. It was now clear to nearly all of the patriots that war with the mother country might be inevitable after all. Increasingly, those colonists who had been either moderate or apathetic started thinking more radically and paying more attention to radical pamphlets. The most influential of these writings was Thomas Paine's *Common Sense*, published in January 1776, which strongly advocated a split with Britain and independence for America. "Everything that is right or reasonable pleads for separation," Paine wrote.

> The blood of the slain, the weeping voice of nature cries, 'TIS TIME TO PART. Even the distance at which the Almighty hath placed England and America is a strong and natural proof

Thomas Paine's influential pamphlet Common Sense *was the first printed work openly to advocate American independence.*

that the authority of the one over the other, was never the design of heaven. . . . Though I would carefully avoid giving unnecessary offense, yet I am inclined to believe, that all those who espouse the doctrine of reconciliation, may be included within the following descriptions. Interested men, who are not to be trusted, weak men who "cannot see, prejudiced men who will not see, and a certain set of moderate men who think better of the European world than it deserves; and this last class, by an ill-judged deliberation, will be the cause of more calamities to this continent than all the other three. . . . 'Tis repugnant to reason, to the universal order of things . . . [to] suppose that this continent can long remain subject to any external power.[25]

By the spring of 1776, not long after Paine's pamphlet appeared, a daring spirit of independence was sweeping through the colonies. As John Adams described it, "Every post [mail delivery] and every day rolls in upon us Independence like a torrent."[26] Radical patriots swiftly gained control of most of the colonial legislatures, and on May 15 the members of the Virginia assembly boldly endorsed the concept of independence. Only three weeks later, one of these men, Richard Henry Lee, took the next logical step and penned a resolution on independence for the Continental Congress to consider and hopefully pass.

Lee's resolution, proposed on June 7, became the chief legal document of American independence. (The Declaration of Independence, soon to follow, was intended only to announce that independence and explain and justify it to the world.) The resolution stated:

Resolved, that these United Colonies are, and of right ought to be, free and independent states, that they are absolved from all allegiance to the British Crown, and that all political connection between them and the state of Great Britain is and ought to be totally dissolved. That it is expedient forthwith to take the most effectual measures for forming foreign alliances. That a plan of confederation be prepared and transmitted to the respective Colonies for their consideration and approbation [approval].[27]

Congress debated Lee's resolution on June 8 and spent more time on it on June 10. There were many crucial issues to consider, especially regarding what Lee had referred to as "effectual measures for forming foreign alliances." All agreed that the colonies, which were minor players at best on the world political stage, could not hope to break free of the mother country without various kinds of aid from foreign powers. An alliance with France was essential, for example. This was because the French had the power to hinder Britain's transport of war supplies. Trade relations with France, Spain, Holland, and other European nations would also be necessary, since the colonies would no longer receive supplies from Britain. Congress also discussed the negative side of such new alliances. For instance, it was possible that France and Spain might see the new American nation as a threat to the considerable North American lands and resources that these nations controlled.

During these debates, it became clear that some of the delegates to Congress were still uncomfortable with the idea of cutting all ties with the mother country. These doubters admitted they were worried that, acting alone, America might lose a war with the British. It might be more prudent, they suggested, to wait until France and a few other strong countries had openly endorsed American independence. In light of this temporary opposition to declaring independence, Lee and his supporters decided to postpone the vote on the resolution for a few weeks. Lee hoped that, given time to reflect on this momentous matter, the doubters would come to see the wisdom of breaking free of Britain sooner rather than later. Jefferson recalled:

JEFFERSON REMEMBERS LEE'S RESOLUTION

In his autobiography (in Adrienne Koch and William Peden's Life and Selected Writings of Thomas Jefferson*), written many years after the American Revolution, Jefferson recalled the circumstances of Lee's resolution for independence this way:*

"The delegates from Virginia moved, in obedience to instructions from their constituents, that the Congress should declare that the United colonies are, and of right ought to be, free and independent states, that they are absolved from all allegiance to the British crown, and that all political connection between them and the state of Great Britain is, and ought to be, totally dissolved."

It appearing in the course of these debates, that the colonies of New York, New Jersey, Pennsylvania, Delaware, Maryland, and South Carolina were not yet matured for falling from the parent stem, but that they were fast advancing to that state, it was thought most prudent to wait a while for them, and to postpone the final decision to July 1st.[28]

JEFFERSON'S MODEST ASSIGNMENT

Lee and the majority of delegates were confident that his resolution for independence would pass in the near future. So on June 11, the day following the temporary shelving of the resolution, Congress appointed a committee to draft a document that would announce and justify American independence. The five members of the committee included Jefferson, Adams, Robert Livingston of New York, Benjamin Franklin of Pennsylvania, and Roger Sherman of Connecticut. These men met and briefly discussed the general form that the document should take.

Then the committee made a decision that, unbeknownst to its members at the time, would eventually have momentous historical consequences. Namely, Adams, Franklin, Livingston, and Sherman asked Jefferson to prepare the crucial initial draft. From a modern vantage, this choice might at first glance seem odd. Of the five men, Jefferson possessed the least experience in Congress and was the least effective orator. Adams, who was an excellent orator and often a leading participant in congressional debates, would have been a much more logical choice to draft such a crucial document. But therein lies the main reason why the others chose Jefferson: At the time, the Declaration was viewed as neither crucial nor any great honor to pen. Also, Adams, Franklin, Sherman, and Livingston were too busy taking part in ongoing debates in Congress. As noted historian Joseph J. Ellis puts it, "Jefferson was asked to draft the

Declaration of Independence in great part because the other eligible authors had more important things to do."[29]

Other evidence demonstrates clearly that Congress did not initially see the Declaration as it is viewed today—as an eternal statement of human rights. Jefferson's modest, somewhat mundane assignment was, for the most part, to do his best to state a concept the patriots already accepted as a fact. Namely, thanks to the recent abuses of the colonies by Britain, America was *already independent of and separate* from the former mother country. Jefferson himself later wrote:

> It was urged by J. Adams . . . and others that no gentleman had argued against the policy or the right of separation from Britain, nor had supposed it possible we should ever renew our connection; that they had only opposed its being now declared. That the question was not whether, by a declaration of independence, we should make ourselves what we are not, but

Although five members comprised the committee to prepare the first draft of the Declaration, the then seemingly unimportant task became Jefferson's sole responsibility.

ADAMS ALSO ASKED TO WRITE THE FIRST DRAFT?

In 1822, some forty-six years after the creation of the Declaration of Independence, patriot John Adams penned this recollection (quoted in volume 1 of Henry Commager and Richard Morris's Spirit of 'Seventy-Six) *of his own role in the drafting process. Modern historians think this account is at the least an exaggeration. In 1823 Thomas Jefferson claimed that the meeting Adams cites never took place and suggested that his aged colleague had "misremembered."*

"The committee met, discussed the subject, and then appointed Mr. Jefferson and me to make the draft, I suppose because we were the two first on the list. The subcommittee [i.e., Adams and Jefferson] met. Jefferson proposed to me to make the draft. I said, 'I will not.' [Jefferson:] 'You should do it.' [Adams:] 'Oh! no.' [Jefferson:] 'Why will you not? You ought to do it.' [Adams:] 'I will not.' [Jefferson:] 'Why?' [Adams:] 'Reason enough.' [Jefferson:] 'What can be your reasons?' [Adams:] 'Reason first—You are a Virginian, and a Virginian ought to appear at the head of this business. Reason second—I am obnoxious, suspected and unpopular. You are very much otherwise. Reason third—You can write ten times better than I can.' 'Well,' said Jefferson, 'if you are decided, I will do as well as I can.'"

whether we should declare a fact that already exists. That as to the Parliament and people of England, we had always been independent of them . . . that so far our connection had been federal only and was now dissolved by the commencement of hostilities. . . . That as to the king, we had been bound to him by allegiance, but that this bond was now dissolved by his assent to the late act of Parliament, by which he declares us out of his protection, and by his levying war on us. . . .

No delegates, then, can be denied, or ever want, a power of declaring an existing truth.[30]

Therefore, when Jefferson retired alone on June 12, 1776, to write the rough draft of the Declaration, neither he nor anyone else expected that a great and timeless document would result. All were in for a surprise. One of history's most profound intellects was about to capture the prevailing American spirit of freedom and independence in a handful of truly memorable phrases.

Chapter

3 Jefferson Writes the Declaration

Thomas Jefferson penned the initial draft of the Declaration of Independence between June 12 and June 28, 1776. He worked in a parlor on the second floor of a house located on the corner of Philadelphia's Seventh and Market Streets. (Jefferson had rented the house from a bricklayer named Jacob Graff.) The folding desk on which he wrote the draft had recently been constructed by a Philadelphia cabinetmaker from Jefferson's own specifications. The writing utensil Jefferson used was a goose quill pen that required redipping in an inkwell after every one or two words, which made the work slow and laborious by modern standards.

These are the basic facts about the mechanical process involved in the creation of one of history's most important documents. Much more complex, fascinating, and sometimes controversial are the sources of Jefferson's ideas for the Declaration. Many books and articles have been written attempting to trace these sources. Some of the sources are fairly obvious, for instance, Jefferson's reliance on the democratic ideals of John Locke and other members of the European intellectual movement known as the Enlightenment. It is also apparent that Jefferson borrowed certain key ideas, and even some words and phrases from fellow Virginian George Mason. Other ideas expressed in the Declaration came from

various other sources, some of them more difficult to identify with certainty. And a few others, of course, came from Jefferson himself.

This thumbnail sketch of the Declaration's sources is bound to surprise some readers. The notion that few of the ideas expressed in the Declaration were original seems to contradict the popular picture of Jefferson, the great founding father and font of wisdom, creating the document completely on his own, from the thin air, so to speak. Yet the Declaration's lack of originality in no way detracts from it or its author. In fact, no great thinker or writer works in isolation; his or her views are always shaped by those of others.

Jefferson was no exception. Like other educated Americans of his day, his worldview was shaped by the political and intellectual ideas current in Europe and America in the seventeenth and eighteenth centuries. It was only natural that Jefferson would draw on these ideas in writing a document intended to state major political and philosophical concepts. "The ideas in the Declaration belonged to everyone and to no one," noted Jefferson biographer Merrill Peterson points out. "They were part of the climate of opinion, and they passed as coin of the realm among American patriots in 1776."[31] In later letters to colleagues, Jefferson himself readily admitted:

Jefferson prepared the first draft of the Declaration in this Philadelphia home, on the corner of Seventh and Market streets.

I did not consider it as any part of my charge to invent new ideas altogether, and to offer no sentiment which had ever been expressed before. . . . The object of the Declaration of Independence [was] not to find out new principles or new arguments never before thought of, not merely to say things which had never been said before; but to place before mankind the common sense of the subject in terms so plain and firm as to command their assent and to justify ourselves in the independent stand we are compelled to take. Neither aiming at originality of principle or sentiment, nor yet copied from any particular and previous writ- ing, it was intended to be an expression of the American mind, and to give to that expression the proper tone and spirit called for by the occasion.[32]

Jefferson's great achievement, therefore, was to combine ideas from diverse sources into a single, coherent, stirring statement of democratic principles.

THE FORM OF JEFFERSON'S ARGUMENT

As Jefferson stood before his desk in his rented room, his first concern was to choose the best format for this statement of principles. He could have chosen a simple, loose format; this would have revealed in the opening sentences that the colonies were declaring their independence and then followed up with a list of reasons. Instead, however, Jefferson chose the format of a syllogism. This is a kind of argument that tries to persuade an audience through simple deductive reasoning. A syllogism consists of three parts: a major premise or idea, stated in an introduction; a minor premise, stated and then developed in the body of the work; and finally a conclusion that follows logically from the first two parts. In a syllogism, therefore, if premise A and premise B are true, the conclusion, C, must be the logical and natural result.

The way that Jefferson applied this format to the document was fairly straightforward. His assignment was to convince the world that the separation of the colonies from Britain was right and justified. To do this, he began with a moral argument that was also a statement of the patriots' daringly democratic political philosophy. His major premise was that just governments are established on equal rights and the consent of the governed. The second paragraph of the initial draft began: "We hold these truths to be sacred and undeniable, that all men are created equal and independent, that from that equal creation they derive rights inherent and inalienable."[33] Further, to ensure that these rights are secure, "governments are instituted among men, deriving their just powers from the consent of the governed." The draft also states that if a government denies its citizens these rights, it is their right to change or dismantle that government and institute a new, fairer one.

The strength of this first premise derives from Jefferson's employment of the phrase "sacred and undeniable." (It was later changed to "self-evident.") Because it was self-evident, it must be a basic moral truth and therefore needed little or no demonstration. Moreover, people of reason and goodwill, no matter what their background or nationality, could be expected immediately to grasp this concept.

For his minor premise, Jefferson charged that the British king, who in the Declaration stood for the whole British government, had consistently denied the "undeniable" rights of the American colonists. Eighteen specific charges followed, including "He has refused his assent to laws, the most wholesome and necessary for the public good"; and "He has kept among us in times of peace standing

Jefferson chose to structure the Declaration as a logical argument in order to convince those who would read it that a split with Britain was justified.

rights, such as equality, and if they do, citizens have the right to abolish said governments. Premise two demonstrated that the British had many times denied the Americans such basic rights. Therefore, following the format of the syllogism (if A and B are true, C must be the result), the Americans were fully justified in splitting with the mother country and declaring "these colonies to be free and independent states."

THE ROOTS OF NATURAL LAW

Having decided on the form the document would take, Jefferson began writing the all-important first premise, his moral argument that certain basic human rights were undeniable. To support this argument, he drew liberally on some of the leading writers of the European Enlightenment. These writers invoked

To support his argument that all humans enjoy basic natural rights, Jefferson turned to the writers of the European Enlightenment.

armies and ships of war without the consent of our legislatures."

In the document's final section, Jefferson related the first premise to the second premise and showed how they led to an inescapable conclusion. In other words, premise one stated that just governments do not deny their citizens basic, inherent

and championed human reason, newly discovered scientific facts, religious toleration, the existence of certain basic natural human rights, and fair government. Enlightenment thinkers contended that science had the potential to show humans how nature worked. If so, people would then possess the means of controlling and exploiting nature to their own advantage. Further, this process would reveal the existence of certain basic natural rights, including freedom of thought, the right of self-expression, and individual personal fulfillment.

Modern civilization was not unique in recognizing these natural rights, the Enlightenment philosophers pointed out. Some two thousand years before, they said, a handful of Greek and Roman thinkers had discussed such ideals. For example, the fourth-century B.C. Greek philosopher Aristotle had talked about the concept of justice. He suggested that in addition to the familiar legal aspects of justice, which differ from place to place, there is a "natural" kind of justice that "has the same validity everywhere." In fact, Aristotle said,

"natural laws are immutable [unchangeable] and have the same validity everywhere (as fire burns both here [i.e., in Greece] and in Persia)."[34] Similarly, the first-century B.C. Roman orator and statesman Cicero argued that a natural, universal law has an unchangeable meaning in nature. True law, he wrote,

> is right reason in harmony with nature. It is spread through the whole human community, unchanging and eternal, calling people to their duty by its commands and deterring them from wrong-doing by its prohibitions.

REVERENCE FOR THE GREEK AND ROMAN MASTERS

The writings of ancient Greek and Roman thinkers, such as Aristotle and Cicero, which are often referred to as the "classics," had a profound effect on the thinking of John Locke and other members of the European Enlightenment. The classics also more directly inspired American thinkers like Jefferson, as explained here by scholar Carl J. Richard (from his book The Founders and the Classics).

"It was mostly in the schools that the founders learned to venerate the classics. The socialization process was so complete, and the classics themselves so attractive, that even bad teachers . . . often instilled a love of literature in their students. . . . The founders loved and respected the classics for the same reason that other people love and respect other traditions: because the classical heritage gave them a sense of identity and purpose, binding them with one another and with their ancestors in a common struggle; and because it supplied them with the intellectual tools necessary to face a violent and uncertain world with some degree of confidence. . . . Throughout their lives, the founders continued to believe that the classics provided an indispensable training in virtue which society could abandon only at its own peril. Hence, most of the founders argued passionately that the educational system must maintain the classical emphasis."

. . . The law [of nature] cannot be countermanded, nor can it be totally . . . rescinded. There will not be one such law in Rome and another in Athens, one now and another in the future, but all peoples in all times will be embraced by a single and eternal and unchangeable [natural] law.[35]

The writers of the European Enlightenment absorbed these and other similar historical arguments about natural rights. They then developed and applied these arguments to the specific political and social conditions of their own time. And this reawakening and rethinking of such concepts steadily and profoundly transformed the way that educated people in Europe and America viewed their political and social institutions.

JEFFERSON'S DEBT TO JOHN LOCKE

The seventeenth-century English philosopher John Locke, for instance, strongly influenced the political ideals of leaders in England, France, and America, including, of course, Jefferson and other patriots. Locke held that traditional societies ruled by absolute monarchs tended to stifle people's natural, basic rights. In his *Two Treatises of Government* (1690), he argued that a government should not be ruled by the arbitrary will of a king. Instead, government should be built on the consent of the people who are governed. In fact, the very function of government should be to preserve people's natural rights, including life, liberty, and property. "To understand political power," Locke wrote,

we must consider what state all men are naturally in, and that is a state of perfect freedom to order their actions and dispose of their possessions . . . as they think fit, within the bounds of the law of nature, without asking leave or depending upon the will of any other man. . . . A state also of equality [is one] wherein all the power and jurisdiction is reciprocal [shared by all], no one having more than another.

Further, said Locke, no person, whether inside or outside of government, has the right to tamper with the law of nature by threatening the life, liberty, or possessions of others. "The state of nature has a law of nature to govern it," he insisted,

which obliges everyone; and reason, which is that law, teaches all mankind . . . that, being equal and independent, no one ought to harm another in his life, health, liberty or possession. . . . And that all men may be restrained from invading others' rights and from doing hurt to one another, and the law of nature be observed, which wills the peace and preservation of all mankind, the execution of the law of nature is, in that state, put into every man's hands. . . . In transgressing the law of nature, the offender declares himself to live by another rule than that of reason and common equity; which is that measure God has set to the actions of men for their mutual security.[36]

It is clear that this and similar passages by Locke inspired Jefferson's use of the words "life," "liberty," "property," and "free and independent" in the Decla-

LEARNING TO THINK LIKE LOCKE

Although Thomas Jefferson, George Mason, and other American thinkers and writers often utilized ideas earlier popularized by Englishman John Locke, they were not directly copying him. The fact is that Locke's ideas were far from new. Copies of his books had been available in the American colonies since before Jefferson was born. Also, American clergymen regularly used Locke's political and moral concepts, along with some of his exact language, in sermons. By the 1770s, Locke's ideas had become so ingrained in men like Jefferson that they tended to draw on them automatically when the situation called for it. The principles and language of Locke's *Second Treatise of Government* were so much a part of Jefferson's and his colleagues' worldview that a number of these men simply came to think and write like Locke.

ration of Independence. Jefferson also borrowed another key concept from Locke. When a government becomes destructive, Jefferson wrote in the initial premise of the Declaration, "it is the right of the people to alter or abolish it." This concept was based directly on Locke's assertion that when rulers threaten or violate the people's rights, the people have the right to rise up against those rulers. According to Locke:

> The end of government is the good of mankind. And which is best for mankind? That the people should be always exposed to the boundless will of tyranny, or that the rulers should be sometimes liable to be opposed when they grow exorbitant [excessive] in the use of their power and employ it for the destruction and not the preservation of the properties of their people?[37]

TOO MUCH POWER IN TOO FEW HANDS

In writing the rough draft of the Declaration, Jefferson drew on other Enlightenment thinkers besides Locke. The great French political philosopher, historian, and jurist Charles de Montesquieu, who had died in 1755, when Jefferson was twelve, also strongly influenced Jefferson and his fellow patriots. Like Locke, Montesquieu came out squarely against tyrannical governments. No matter how well intentioned a people and a government might be, the Frenchman warned, there was always a danger of that government becoming tyrannical if too much power rested in the hands of only a few individuals.

In forming a government, therefore, the people should separate the various branches; they should also balance the powers of these branches so that no single branch can dominate the others. In his 1748 treatise, *The Spirit of the Laws*, Montesquieu stated that a just government must be divided into three fully independent parts, the legislative, executive, and judicial. "When legislative power is united with executive power in a single person or in a single body of the magistracy," he said,

> there is no liberty, because one can fear that the same monarch or senate that makes tyrannical laws will execute them tyrannically. Nor is there liberty if the power of judging is not separate from legislative power and from exec-

Enlightenment thinker Charles de Montesquieu advocated the division of government powers through a system of checks and balances.

utive power. If it were joined to legislative power, the power over the life and liberty of the citizens would be arbitrary [subject to the whims of the powerful], for the judge would be the legislator. If it were joined to executive power, the judge could have the force of an oppressor. All would be lost if the same man or the same body of principal men . . . exercised these three powers, that of making laws, that of executing public resolutions, and that of judging the crimes or the disputes of individuals.[38]

In writing the Declaration, Jefferson did not directly discuss such separation of governmental powers. Yet he did refer to Montesquieu's ideas indirectly. The following words appear in the Declaration's second paragraph:

> Whenever any form of government becomes destructive . . . it is the right of the people to alter or to abolish it, and to institute new government, laying its foundation on such principles and organizing its powers in such form, as to them shall seem most likely to effect their safety and happiness.[39]

The phrase "organizing its powers in such form" referred to the separation of powers advocated by Montesquieu. The notion of separation of powers is indirectly invoked again in the Declaration in the passage in which Jefferson enumerates the abuses of the British king. Listing these wrongs, perpetrated by what the Americans viewed as a tyrannical monarchy, demonstrated that in the mother country too much power rested in too few hands. The implication was that, in forming their new government, the Americans would avoid this situation by separating and balancing the powers of the governmental branches.

INFLUENCES OF AMERICAN WRITERS

It is essential to emphasize that not all of the ideas, words, and phrases presented in the Declaration of Independence came directly from Locke, Montesquieu, and other members of the European Enlightenment. Most American leaders were highly educated themselves. And some, like Jefferson, George Mason, and Benjamin Franklin, were gifted thinkers and writers in their own right. In a very real sense, these American intellectuals deserve to be classified as members of a new branch of the Enlightenment—the American branch.

One American intellectual whom Jefferson borrowed heavily from in writing the Declaration was himself. Indeed, various words, phrases, and even whole sentences in the document derived from his own earlier writings. Particularly striking are similarities to the preamble he had written for the new constitution of Virginia in May 1776, only weeks before beginning work on the Declaration. A list of grievances against King George III appears in the preamble; and a number of these grievances made their way into the Declaration with only minor changes.

In the Virginia document, for instance, Jefferson wrote that the king had denied "his governors permission to pass laws of immediate and pressing importance, unless suspended in their operation for his assent, and, when so suspended, neglecting to attend to them for many years." The somewhat-amended version in the Declaration reads: "He has forbidden his governors to pass laws of immediate and pressing importance, unless suspended in their operation till his assent should be obtained; and when so suspended, he has utterly neglected to attend to them." Another grievance made the transition from one document to the other almost unchanged. In the Virginia document: "By plundering our seas, ravaging our coasts, burning our towns, and destroying the lives of our people."[40] In the Declaration: "He has plundered our seas, ravaged our coasts, burnt our towns, and destroyed the lives of our people."[41]

Jefferson's debt to fellow Virginian George Mason is also apparent from a close examination of the Declaration and Mason's writings. In particular, Jefferson borrowed a number of words and phrases from the bill of rights that Mason penned for the Virginia Constitution shortly before Jefferson wrote the Declaration. Mason wrote that

> all men are by nature equally free and independent, and have certain inherent rights . . . namely, the enjoyment of life and liberty, with the means of acquiring and possessing property, and pursuing and obtaining happiness and safety.[42]

In comparison, Jefferson wrote in the draft of the opening of the Declaration that

> all men are created equal and independent; that from that equal creation

WHY NO MENTION OF PARLIAMENT?

The list of grievances in the Declaration of Independence makes no mention of Parliament, which was most responsible for the abuses endured by the colonies in the years leading up to the Declaration. In this excerpt from his acclaimed book on the Declaration, scholar Carl Becker explains why.

"So striking an omission must have been intentional. It was of course impossible to make out a list of grievances against Great Britain without referring to such acts as the Stamp Act . . . the Boston Port Bill, and many other legislative measures. And the framers of the Declaration . . . had accordingly to . . . avoid naming the Parliament that passed them. . . . The framers . . . refrained from mentioning Parliament . . . for the same reason that they charged all their grievances against the king alone. Being now committed to independence, the position of the colonies could not be simply or convincingly presented from the point of view of the rights of British subjects [who legally would owe allegiance to Parliament]. . . . Separation from Great Britain was therefore justified on more general grounds, on the ground of the natural rights of man. And in order to simplify the issue . . . it was expedient that these rights should seem to be as little as possible limited or obscured by the . . . legal obligations [including those to Parliament] that were admittedly binding upon British subjects."

they derive rights inherent and inalienable, among which are the preservation of life, and liberty, and the pursuit of happiness.[43]

A "MELTING POT OF IDEAS AND PHRASES"

One should not conclude from this comparison that Jefferson had no good ideas of his own and in desperation turned to plagiarizing Mason. The fact is that most of these words, as well as the ideas behind them, were not original with either Mason *or* Jefferson. They came from a sort of melting pot of ideas and phrases contributed to by many writers on both sides of the Atlantic and that were then current, familiar to, and discussed by all of the American patriots.

Jefferson himself later admitted to borrowing from this melting pot. In a May

1825 letter to a colleague, he stated that the authority of the Declaration rested on "the harmonizing sentiments of the day, whether expressed in conversation, in letters, printed essays, or in the elementary books of public right, as Aristotle, Cicero, Locke," and others. "The historical documents" written by these men "you will find to be corroborative of [supportive of and in agreement with] the facts and principles advanced in [the] Declaration."[44]

Thus, the various similarities between the sentiments in Mason's Virginia bill of rights and Jefferson's Declaration are the result of the two men drawing on the same pool of ideas. Take, for instance, the following statement by Mason in the Virginia document:

> Government is, and ought to be, instituted for the common benefit, protection, and security, of the people, nation, or community. . . . Whenever any government shall be found inadequate or contrary to these purposes, a majority of the community hath an . . . inalienable . . . right, to reform, alter, or abolish it.[45]

In a like manner, Jefferson wrote in the Declaration:

> Governments are instituted among men, deriving their just powers from the consent of the governed. . . . Whenever any form of government becomes destructive of these ends, it is the right of the people to alter or to abolish it.[46]

Rather than copying Mason, Jefferson was paraphrasing a widely circulated and accepted idea that had come originally from Europe. "The fundamental claim that revolution is justified if the existent rulers demonstrate systematic disregard for the rights of their subjects certainly originated with Locke," Joseph Ellis points out. "Jefferson may have gotten his specific language from George Mason, but both men knew whom they were paraphrasing."[47]

Still another prominent concept that Jefferson derived from the contemporary intellectual melting pot is that human beings have an inherent right to happiness. A number of European thinkers had written that a just government was one that guaranteed its people's happiness. In his Virginia bill of rights, George Mason

While drafting the Declaration, Jefferson borrowed heavily from the writings of his colleague, George Mason.

asserted that the best government was that "which is capable of producing the greatest degree of happiness and safety."[48] In his treatise *The Rights of Man*, Thomas Paine insisted that among the natural human rights are "those rights of acting as an individual for his own comfort and happiness."[49] And John Adams referred to the right to happiness five times in the constitution he drafted for his home state of Massachusetts. It is hardly surprising, therefore, that Jefferson also addressed this issue in the rough draft of the Declaration of Independence. All people are endowed with certain basic rights, he stated, and "among these are life, liberty, and the pursuit of happiness."[50]

The sources of Jefferson's ideas for the Declaration were many and varied, therefore. Yet the document is much more than a mere collection of borrowed concepts. Jefferson's singular, unusually prodigious intellect and education acted as a sort of clearinghouse for these concepts, an anvil on which he accepted and reshaped some, melted down and reforged others, and totally discarded still others. The result was a carefully crafted statement of liberty and human rights that drew on many other writers, yet was also unique to Jefferson. Its genius took his colleagues by pleasant surprise; and it remains, unarguably, one of the most sublime achievements of the human mind.

4 Revising and Ratifying the Declaration

When Jefferson finished writing the rough draft of the Declaration in late June 1776, he was well aware that this was not the final product. First, he would have to show the document to the other members of the drafting committee. They would no doubt make revisions. That second draft would then go to Congress, which would debate its merits and make further alterations. For the moment, Jefferson had no way of foreseeing how extensive these changes might be.

and amendments I wished most to have the benefit before presenting it to the committee.[51]

The three men met at least twice and made a total of twenty-six revisions. Unfortunately, their exact reasons for these changes will always remain unknown. They simply did not anticipate that the document would come to be revered and

Benjamin Franklin and John Adams review Jefferson's first draft of the Declaration.

REVIEW BY THE COMMITTEE

Shortly before June 28, Jefferson sent word to the other members of the drafting committee that he was ready to show them the fruits of his labor. Franklin and Adams were the first to see the document. "Before I reported it to the committee," Jefferson later recalled,

> I communicated it *separately* to Dr. Franklin and Mr. Adams, requesting their corrections, because they were the two members of whose judgments

SEVERAL ELECTRIFYING PHRASES

Admirers of the Declaration of Independence have often pointed out the mastery with which Jefferson expressed the core essences of human dignity and democratic theory in simple terms that anyone anywhere could readily comprehend. These terms took the form of several noble and electrifying phrases, one following closely on another, especially in the document's opening and closing paragraphs. Among them are: "The course of human events," "all men are created equal," "life, liberty, and the pursuit of happiness," "just powers from the consent of the governed," "the right of the people," "the voice of justice," "hold them, as we hold the rest of mankind," "appealing to the supreme judge of the world," "our lives, our fortunes, and our sacred honor." In a document containing fewer than fifteen hundred words, historian Merrill D. Peterson points out in his biography of Jefferson, its author managed to present a worldview, a political philosophy, and a national creed. "This was a triumph. It raised the American cause above parochialism [narrow, local concerns], above history, and united it with the cause of mankind. A philosophy of human rights attained timeless symbolization in words that inspired action; action became thought and thought became action."

that future generations of Americans would desire to know every motive, word, and thought in its drafting process. So they kept no notes or other record of their meetings. What is certain is that of the twenty-six revisions, twenty-three were changes in wording, two of them in Adams's handwriting, five in Franklin's, and sixteen in Jefferson's. The other three changes were brief paragraphs added to the text.

One of Franklin's revisions slightly amended the section in which Jefferson charged that the king "has made our judges dependent on his will alone, for the tenure of their offices, and amount of their salaries."[52] Franklin altered the wording to "and the amount and payment of their salaries." Another of Franklin's revisions affected the section reading: "but when a long train of abuses and usurpations . . . evinces a design to reduce them to arbitrary power, it is their right . . . to throw off such government." Franklin changed the words "to arbitrary power" to "under absolute despotism."

Of Adams's revisions, one occurred in the section that charged that the king "has dissolved representative houses repeatedly. . . . He has refused for a long space of time to cause others to be elected." Adams added the phrase "after such dissolutions" after the word "time."

Jefferson's own initial revisions included some new paragraphs, perhaps suggested by either Franklin or Adams. One of these paragraphs, which Jefferson jotted down on a slip of paper, read: "He [the king] has called together legislative bodies at places unusual, uncomfortable, and distant from the depository of their public records, for the sole purpose of fatiguing them into compliance with his measures." Jefferson pasted the slip of paper to the rough draft so that the new paragraph immediately preceded the words "He [the king] has dissolved representative houses repeatedly and continually."

Once these few initial revisions had been made, Livingston and Sherman examined the rough draft. No evidence suggests that they made any changes of their own. Satisfied that the draft, which they referred to as the "fair copy," was ready for the next step in the review process, the committee members submitted it to Congress on June 28.

MINOR REVISIONS BY CONGRESS

At that particular moment, however, the Declaration was not foremost on the minds of the delegates. So they temporarily set it aside. Their attention was presently riveted on debating and voting on Lee's resolution for independence. On July 1, the first vote was taken on the resolution. The count was nine "yes" and four "abstain." The colonies that abstained did so because debate on the resolution was still going on in their separate legislatures. So discussion continued in Congress throughout the day on July 1 and during the morning of July 2. The historic final vote took place in the

afternoon of July 2. After New York became the last colony to vote "yes," approval for the colonies breaking free of the mother country was unanimous. Lee's resolution was the legal statement of independence. So, contrary to later popular belief, July 2, 1776, and *not* July 4, was the day that the United States was officially born.

Following the passage of Lee's resolution, the next order of business for Congress was the debate on the Declaration of Independence. Discussion and revision began late in the afternoon of July 2 and continued for almost three solid days. During this intensive marathon session, Congress made a number of changes, including the deletion of about a quarter of the text.

Some of these changes were fairly minor. For example, Jefferson had written in the rough draft: "and such is now the necessity which constrains them [the colonies] to expunge their former systems of governments." For the word "expunge," Congress substituted "alter." The exact reason for this change is uncertain, but it was probably a matter of clarity and readability. As it remains today, the word "expunge" was literary and somewhat obscure. The founders wanted the Declaration to make a simple, powerful statement that would be easily readable and understood by people everywhere. And "alter" was much simpler and clearer than "expunge."[53]

Also, Jefferson had written: "The history of the present king of Great Britain is a history of unremitting injuries and usurpations." Congress replaced the word "unremitting" with "repeated." In this case, the members of Congress likely felt that "unremitting" was not quite accurate

CELEBRATING JULY 2?

In early July 1776, the founders viewed the Declaration mainly as a formality, a convenient announcement of and justification for independence. They did not foresee that the document would become revered or that the date of its approval would come to be celebrated as the nation's Independence Day. At the time, they thought July 2, the day Lee's resolution passed, would become America's birthday, as illustrated in this excerpt from a letter John Adams sent his wife on July 3, quoted in his Diary and Autobiography:

"Yesterday the greatest question was decided which ever was debated in America, and a greater, perhaps, never was nor will be decided among men. A resolution was passed without one dissenting colony, 'that these United Colonies are, and of right ought to be, free and independent States.' . . . The second day of July, 1776, will be the most memorable epocha [event beginning a new era] in the history of America. I am apt to believe that it will be celebrated by succeeding generations as the great anniversary festival. It ought to be commemorated as the day of deliverance. . . . It ought to be solemnized with pomp and parade, with shows, games, sports, guns, bells, bonfires and illuminations [fireworks], from one end of this continent to the other, from this time forward, forevermore."

Most Founding Fathers believed that future generations would celebrate July 2 as America's birthday.

because it implied that the "injuries" inflicted by the British had occurred constantly, without any pause. Using "repeated" made it clear that the injuries took place periodically.[54]

Another type of minor revision was the addition of new words and phrases. In general, this was done to clarify or emphasize a point. For instance, the list of abuses in the rough draft included one that charged the king with "giving assent" to acts "for depriving us of the benefits of trial by jury." Congress concluded that the existing phrase might be interpreted to mean that the British had denied the colonists their right to trial by jury in "all cases." In reality, this abuse had been inconsistent, occurring in some places and times but not in others. Therefore, the delegates added the words "in many cases." This rendered the fairer and more accurate charge: "for depriving us in many cases of the benefits of trial by jury."[55]

Congress also sought to make some of Jefferson's original statements more forceful. For example, in the rough draft he had accused the king of "transporting large armies . . . to complete the works of death, desolation and tyranny already begun with circumstances of cruelty and perfidy [treachery] unworthy the head of a civilized nation." Congress decided that this statement did not express enough outrage that the British had unleashed troops on American towns. As a solution, the delegates inserted nine new words, which resulted in this much stronger wording: "to complete the works of death, desolation and tyranny already begun with circumstances of cruelty and perfidy scarcely paralleled in the most barbarous ages, and totally unworthy the head of a civilized nation."[56]

MAJOR REVISIONS BY CONGRESS

Congress also made some more substantial revisions to Jefferson's rough draft. In most cases, these changes consisted of the deletion of whole paragraphs. Motivating the delegates in making these alterations was a concern that certain passages in the rough draft might offend those British legislators and citizens who were sympathetic to the American cause. For example, one of Jefferson's original passages called British leaders "the disturbers of our harmony." Further, said Jefferson, these members of Parliament had enacted many abusive laws (among them the Stamp Act and Intolerable Acts), which had proved injurious to the colonies. British leaders had also sent "not only soldiers of our common blood, but Scotch and foreign mercenaries to invade and deluge us in blood."[57]

In retaliation for these acts, Jefferson had written, it was necessary for the Americans to "renounce forever these unfeeling brethren," and "to forget our former love for them and to hold them as we hold the rest of mankind, [as] enemies in war, in peace friends." In an almost emotional touch of regret, Jefferson then reminded the British of what they had thrown away. "We might have been a free and great people together," he said. However, showing the colonists understanding and respect was "below their [i.e., British] dignity." So, said Jefferson, "we will climb" the road to happiness and glory "apart from them," in "eternal separation."[58]

Uneasy about these blunt statements, many members of Congress suggested that they be either toned down or deleted. It would be more prudent, they said, to focus all of their indignation and anger on the king, who was in a very real sense more of a symbol than a person. Jefferson was unhappy about these deletions, feeling that there was no need for the patriots to worry about being polite. "The pusillanimous [timid] idea that we had friends in England worth keeping terms with, still haunted the minds of many," he later recalled. "For this reason, those passages which conveyed censures [criticisms] on the people of England were struck out, lest they should give them offense."[59]

JEFFERSON'S ATTACK ON SLAVERY

These cuts did not upset Jefferson nearly as much as Congress's wholesale deletion of his bold denunciation of the slave trade. Although he himself owned slaves, Jefferson viewed the institution as morally wrong. (A question often asked over the years is, If Jefferson was morally against slavery, why did he not free his own slaves? Among the various reasons historians have proposed, the most credible is that he feared that they would suffer deprivations due to the lack of economic opportunities for free blacks at the time, as well as prejudice, social rejection, and other such cruelties. He therefore felt his slaves were better off remaining in his charge, where they would be well treated and free from want.) From a practical standpoint, Jefferson realized, slavery was extremely entrenched in American society and would be difficult to dislodge. However, he believed that the epic event of starting a new country was the perfect opportunity to remove the repugnant institution, which would allow the Americans to begin anew without slaves.

In fact, Jefferson was not the only American leader who felt that slavery was wrong and should be done away with. Less than a year after he wrote the Declaration, the Massachusetts legislature considered a widely popular antislavery petition that read in part:

Your petitioners apprehend that they [black people] have in common with all other men a natural and unalienable right to that freedom which the Great Parent of the Universe [i.e., God] has bestowed equally on all mankind and which they have never forfeited by any compact or agreement whatever—but that [they] were unjustly dragged by the hand of cruel power from their dearest friends and some of them even torn from the embraces of their tender parents—from a populous, pleasant and plentiful country and in violation of [the] laws of nature and of nations . . . brought here . . . to be sold like beasts of burden. . . . Your petitioners have long and patiently waited . . . but with grief [they] reflect that . . . it has never been considered that every principle from which America has acted in the course of [its] unhappy difficulties with Great Britain pleads stronger than a thousand arguments in favor of your petitioners . . . who humbly beseech your honors to . . . [pass an act that would restore blacks] to the enjoyments of that [freedom] which is the natural right of all men.[60]

Even stronger was the moral stand Jefferson took against the slave trade in

CONGRESS TONES DOWN JEFFERSON'S ATTACK

This is Congress's complete revision of the sections of the rough draft in which Jefferson had strongly criticized the British people (available in Carl Becker's book about the Declaration). The deleted passages are both italicized and bracketed and the additions are in uppercase.

"Nor have we been wanting in attentions to our British brethren. We have warned them from time to time of attempts by their legislature to extend AN UNWARRANTABLE [*a*] jurisdiction over US [*these our states*]. We have reminded them of the circumstances of our emigration and settlement here, [*no one of which could warrant so strange a pretension: that these were effected at the expense of our own blood and treasure, unassisted by the wealth or the strength of Great Britain: that in constituting indeed our several forms of government, we had adopted one common king, thereby laying a foundation for perpetual league and amity with them; but that submission to their parliament was no part of our constitution, nor ever in idea, if history may be credited: and,*] we HAVE appealed to their native justice and magnanimity AND WE HAVE CONJURED THEM BY [*as well as to*] the ties of our common kindred to disavow these usurpations which WOULD INEVITABLY [*were likely to*] interrupt our connection and correspondence. They too have been deaf to the voice of justice and consanguinity. WE MUST THEREFORE [*and when occasions have been given them, by the regular course of their laws, of removing from their councils the disturbers of our harmony, they have, by their free election, re-established them in power. At this very time too, they are permitting their chief magistrate to send over not only soldiers of our common blood, but Scotch and foreign mercenaries to invade and destroy us. These facts have given the last stab to agonizing affection, and manly spirit bids us to renounce forever these unfeeling brethren. We must endeavor to forget our former love for them, and hold them as we would hold the rest of mankind, enemies in war, in peace friends. We might have been a free and great people together; but a communication of grandeur and of freedom, it seems, is below their dignity. Be it so, since they will have it. The road to happiness and to glory is open to us, too. We will tread it apart from them, and*] acquiesce in the necessity which denounces our [*eternal*] separation. AND HOLD THEM AS WE HOLD THE REST OF MANKIND, ENEMIES IN WAR, IN PEACE FRIENDS!"

Although Jefferson wrote a passage in the Declaration condemning the institution of slavery, it was omitted from the final draft of the document.

the rough draft of the Declaration. The controversial deleted passage reads:

> He [the king] has waged cruel war against human nature itself, violating its most sacred rights of life and liberty in the persons of a distant people who never offended him [i.e., black Africans], captivating and carrying them into slavery in another hemisphere, or to incur miserable death in their transportation thither [from there to here]. This piratical warfare, the opprobrium [disgraceful conduct] of infidel powers, is the warfare of the Christian king of Great Britain, determined to keep open a market where men should be bought and sold, he has prostituted his

negative for suppressing every legislative attempt to prohibit or to restrain this execrable [repulsive] commerce: and that this assemblage of horrors might want no fact of distinguished die, he is now exciting those very people [the slaves] to rise in arms against us, and to purchase that liberty of which he has deprived them, by murdering the people upon whom he also obtruded [forced] them; thus paying off former crimes committed against the liberties of one people, with the crimes which he urges them to commit against the lives of another.[61]

John Adams, who disliked slavery as much as Jefferson, had been pleased when he had first seen this courageous attack on the slave trade. By contrast, when the delegates from the southern states saw it, they were shocked and disturbed. They fervently objected to the passage and vowed to block any interruption of the trade. Adams later wrote:

> I was delighted with its [the Declaration's] high tone and the flights of oratory with which it abounded, especially that concerning Negro slavery, which, though I knew his Southern brethren would never suffer to pass in Congress, I certainly would never oppose. . . . But they [the delegates] obliterated some of the best of it [the rough draft]. . . . I have long wondered that the original draft had not been published. I suppose the reason is the vehement philippic [forceful attack] against Negro slavery.[62]

For the rest of his life, Jefferson regretted the deletion of the antislavery passage. Undaunted, however, he remained committed to hindering the slave trade any way he could. (In the fall of 1776, he introduced a bill in the Virginia legislature calling for a ban on the importation of slaves to that state. The bill passed into law two years later. Although this did not stop Virginians from owning slaves, it was an important step in the long process of eliminating the slavery institution altogether.)

HOW JEFFERSON SAW THE REVISION PROCESS

During Congress's three days of discussions and revisions of the Declaration's rough draft, Jefferson sat quietly in his seat. He later recalled, "I thought it my duty to be, on that occasion, a passive auditor of the opinions of others, more impartial judges than I could be, of its merits and demerits."[63] But though Jefferson was quiet, he was not by any means completely passive. Though he tried not to show his discomfort, he squirmed and sighed and contorted his face, feeling that many of the changes that his colleagues were making in the document bordered on butchery. He was so upset that years later, in writing his autobiography, he made sure to include the Declaration's first draft, word for word, so that future generations would know his original intentions. According to Joseph Ellis:

> For his part, Jefferson went out of his way to disavow responsibility for the version of the Declaration passed by Congress. His own version, he explained to friends back in Virginia, had

been badly treated (the operative word was "mangled"). . . . He needed to differentiate between his language and the published version being circulated throughout the country, claiming that Congress had watered down the purity of his message in order to appease the faint of heart, who still hoped for reconciliation with England. Although this was hardly the case—the revisions of the draft were driven less by desire to compromise than to clarify—Jefferson maintained a wounded sense of betrayal by the Congress throughout the remainder of his life.[64]

Despite this general bitterness toward Congress as a whole, Jefferson later recalled with pride that not all of his colleagues were quick to alter the rough draft of the Declaration of Independence. His friend John Adams, whose voice in the debate was one of the loudest, constantly endeavored to keep the original document intact. "I will say [this] about Mr. Adams," Jefferson wrote to fellow founder James Madison in August 1823, "that he supported the Declaration with zeal and ability, fighting fearlessly for every word of it."[65]

While Adams was defending the rough draft, Benjamin Franklin noticed its author's intense discomfort and sat down beside Jefferson. "I was sitting by Dr. Franklin," Jefferson wrote in the same letter to Madison,

> who perceived that I was not insensible to these mutilations [of the Declaration's rough draft]. And it was on that occasion, that by way of comfort, he told me the story of John Thompson, the hatter [hatmaker] and his new sign.[66]

Franklin's story (constituting the longest of Jefferson's recollections of the Declaration's revision process) went as follows:

> I have made it a rule, whenever [it is] in my power, to avoid becoming the draftsman of papers to be reviewed by a public body. I took my lesson from an incident which I will relate to you. When I was a journeyman printer, one of my companions, an apprentice hatter, having served out his time, was about to open shop for himself. His first concern was to have a handsome sign-board, with a proper inscription. He composed it in these words, "John Thompson, *Hatter, makes* and *sells hats* for ready money," with a figure of a hat subjoined [attached]; but he thought he would submit it to his friends for their amendments. The first he showed it to thought the word *"Hatter"* tautologous [needlessly repetitive], because [it was] followed by the words "makes hats," which showed he was a hatter. It was struck out. The next [of the hatter's friends] observed that the word *"makes"* might as well be omitted, because his customers would not care who made the hats. If [the hats were] good and to their mind, they would buy [them], by whomsoever [they were] made. He struck it out. A third [friend] said he thought the words *"for ready money"* [i.e., cash] were useless, as it was not the custom of the place to sell on credit. Everyone

who purchased [a hat] expected to pay [cash]. [These words] were parted with, and the inscription now stood, "John Thompson sells hats." "*Sells hats!*" says his next friend. Why nobody will expect you to give them away, [so] what then is the use of that word? It was stricken out, and "*hats*" followed it, the rather [since] there was one painted on the board. So the inscription was reduced ultimately to "John Thompson" with the figure of a hat subjoined.[67]

Thanks in part to Franklin, Jefferson managed to survive the debate and revision process without losing his composure. From a modern vantage, the revisions that so upset Jefferson actually largely helped rather than hurt the document. Today most scholars feel that the revisions made the Declaration clearer, more understandable, and actually stronger in its impact. "Congress corrected him precisely where he had allowed himself to go astray," writes noted historian Merrill D. Peterson. Jefferson's colleagues fixed his more "wordy statements" and cumbersome language. "Cleared of these aberrations, the intrinsic [inherent] merits of the work stood in bolder relief than when it passed from Jefferson's hands." Furthermore, the greatness of the document eventually became apparent to people around the world. This benefited Jefferson and his reputation because "in the longer run of time, Jefferson's destiny rode with it."[68]

Benjamin Franklin comforted Jefferson as Congress revised his Declaration.

THE MYTHICAL AND REAL SIGNING CEREMONIES

The revision of the Declaration of Independence finally concluded late in the day on July 4, 1776. In later years, paintings and films tended to reenact a subsequent ceremony held that same day, in which all of the delegates to Congress stepped up in dramatic fashion and signed the Declaration. Perhaps the most famous version of the scene is artist John Trumbull's magnificent 1817 oil painting that now graces the rotunda of the U.S. Capitol building in Washington, D.C. (Trumbull claimed to have based his depiction of the faces of many of the founders on sketches of them he did from life.)

Unfortunately, this stirring vision of the signing ceremony is a popular myth.

John Trumbull's famous oil painting shows members of Congress stepping forward to sign the Declaration of Independence on July 4, 1776.

The actual signing was much more complicated and drawn out. As Thomas Fleming points out:

> Historians still debate whether anyone besides President [of the Congress] John Hancock signed the Declaration on July 4, 1776. . . . A majority of scholars are now inclined to believe no signatures [except for that of Hancock himself] were added until [later] . . . when, by the Congress's order, it had been "engrossed on parchment." . . . One reason for the slow pace may have been Jefferson's final words [in

the document], which required everyone who signed to "mutually pledge to each other our lives, our fortunes and our sacred honor." This was not an overstatement. Everyone was keenly aware that the Declaration of Independence was treason. When John Hancock placed his large scrawl at the head of the document, he reportedly said, "We must be unanimous; there must be no pulling different ways; we must all hang together." "Yes," Benjamin Franklin replied. "We must all hang together. Or most assuredly we shall all hang separately."[69]

The most convincing reconstruction of the ratification and signing process is as follows. After debate and revision of the document concluded on July 4, all of the states except for New York agreed to adopt the Declaration as an announcement of American independence. The New York legislature did not officially accept the document until July 15, at which time ratification became unanimous.

In the meantime, sometime between July 5 and 7, an unknown number of copies of the Declaration were printed and distributed to the state legislatures. George Washington and other leading military officers also received copies. According to John Adams (in a passage in one of his later letters), the initial public reading of the Declaration occurred in the yard of Philadelphia's statehouse, where a large crowd had gathered. After the ceremony, the local militia paraded to the town common and bells rang through most of the night. This same scene, with only minor variations, was reenacted all across America in the weeks that followed.

These first printed copies of the Declaration bore no signatures, except perhaps for John Hancock's (and possibly that of Charles Thomson, the congressional secretary). On July 19, Congress ordered the document to be copied to parchment and signed by the congressional delegates. Because most of these men had dispersed to their various states and had to reassemble for the occasion, the formal signing ceremony did not occur until August 2. Jefferson likely signed on that date. A number of his colleagues were unable to make it to the ceremony, however. Therefore, they ended up affixing their signatures over the course of the ensuing few days and weeks. Fifty-six members of Congress signed it in all, although their signatures were not made public until January 1777.

As a written document, the Declaration was destined to go on to an eventful and colorful historical life in the following two centuries. By contrast, the sentiments expressed in that document were inflammatory and dangerous when first made public. They ensured that the American patriots would have to fight the most powerful nation on Earth in order to achieve the independence they had so daringly declared.

Chapter

5 The War to Enforce the Declaration

Beginning in July and August 1776, people in villages and towns throughout the former British colonies gathered in town squares to hear public readings of the Declaration of Independence. They were fully aware that Congress's issuing of the document was no formal war declaration. Everyone knew that the war had, for all intents and purposes, started months before. The Battles of Concord, Lexington, and Bunker Hill, as well as King George's announcement that the colonies were in open rebellion and would be dealt with, had firmly set the conflict in motion. The Declaration was, in a sense, an afterthought. In defiant terms, it told the king and Parliament that the colonists were not only determined to continue resisting; henceforward they were going to do so as independent Americans rather than as rebellious British.

This defiant and patriotic attitude was apparent in the celebrations in the town squares. In Savannah, Georgia, for example, local patriots read the document at least three times in one day. According to an eyewitness:

After the reading of the Declaration [twice], [local militiamen] discharged their field pieces and fired in platoons. Upon this they proceeded to the Battery [artillery area] . . . where

the Declaration was read for the last time, and the cannon of the Battery discharged. . . . Everyone dined . . . and cheerfully drank to the United Free and Independent States of America . . . My friends and fellow citizens . . . let us remember that America is free and independent; that she is, and will be, with the blessing of the Almighty, great among the nations of the earth. . . . May God give us blessing, and let all the people say Amen![70]

The many Americans who celebrated their newfound independence in this manner had good reason to be proud. The potential existed for them to build a strong, free, and great nation offering numerous opportunities to its citizens. Yet they had just as much reason to be fearful. The Declaration had announced American independence to a watching world, but the document had no way of guaranteeing American freedom, no way of enforcing its bold and defiant rebuke against the mother country. The naked truth was that Great Britain was the most powerful nation and empire on Earth. Most people in Europe, and a good many in America, were sure that the American patriots had no hope of winning the coming conflict. Even Jefferson, Adams, Lee, Franklin, Washington, and their supporters fully realized that they faced a difficult uphill fight; they also knew that if they lost, the Declaration would become little more than a piece of paper trampled into the dirt by the boots of victorious British troops.

THE ODDS AGAINST THE PATRIOTS

The case against an American victory in a war with Britain was made by reputable leaders on both sides of the Atlantic. General Gage, who had ordered his troops to march on Concord in April 1775, summed up the most prevalent British view. "What fools you are," he said, addressing patriot leaders directly, "to pretend to resist the power of Great Britain." During the French and Indian War, he pointed out, Britain had kept three hundred thousand men under arms. "[She] will do the same now rather than suffer the ungrateful people of this country to continue in their rebellion."[71] A respected New Yorker, Charles Inglis, one of many prominent Americans who opposed independence, agreed with Gage. "Devastation and ruin must mark the progress of this war," Inglis wrote shortly before the publication of the Declaration of Independence.

> Hitherto [before this], Britain has not exerted her power. Her number of troops and ships of war here at present is very little more than she judged expedient in time of peace. . . . But as soon as

we declare for independence, every prospect of this kind must vanish. Ruthless war, with all its aggravated horrors, will ravage our once happy land; our seacoasts and ports will be ruined, and our ships taken. Torrents of blood will be spilled and thousands [of people] reduced to beggary and wretchedness.[72]

Gage, Inglis, and others who thought America had no chance in the war pointed out that the British advantage in manpower alone was overwhelming. This

A crowd gathers to listen as Colonel John Nixon reads the Declaration from the balcony of Philadelphia's Independence Hall on July 8, 1776.

observation often proved accurate as the conflict unfolded. At any given time, Britain had more than thirty thousand troops engaged in various operations against the Americans. American forces, in contrast, were always much smaller. At its largest, the Continental army commanded by George Washington consisted of twenty thousand regular soldiers. Most of these men signed up to serve for several months at most, however; and there were many casualties and deserters. So Washington frequently found himself with as few as five thousand regulars at his disposal. (The state militias often

British General Thomas Gage believed that American resistance was futile.

aided the regulars, at times very effectively. However, they were haphazardly organized and lacked the training and discipline of many American and British regulars.)

An even more decisive advantage for Britain was its superiority on the seas. The British navy was the world's largest. In the summer of 1776, Britain had twenty-eight large warships in American waters, vessels that could effectively blockade U.S. ports and ferry British troops swiftly from one place to another. The British also had many warships elsewhere that could reach America within a few weeks at most. More than a hundred of these vessels were equipped with between sixty and a hundred powerful cannons.

The Americans had no formal navy to counter this formidable threat. None of their ships had cannons, and initially all they could muster were a few dozen small schooners (sailboats) and cargo ships. Congress did quite wisely establish the Continental navy, which implemented a crash program for building warships; however, these vessels were far fewer in number and carried fewer cannons than the British ships they would have to fight. (These disadvantages became painfully clear when the British burned or captured most of the new American warships by 1779.)

Still another logistical difficulty faced by the American patriots was the existence of large numbers of Loyalists, not only in 1776 but throughout the war. About 850,000 of North America's inhabitants were Loyalists, fully a third of the total population. Moreover, these British sympathizers were scattered widely, in every city and town and throughout the countryside. Many of them viewed the

One common argument against the colonies going to war with Britain was that America lacked the necessary military resources. For example, Jacob Duché, rector of Christ's Church in Philadelphia, wrote this message (quoted in Catherine S. Crary's The Price of Loyalty) *to George Washington, begging him to refrain from fighting.*

"Where are your resources? O my dear sir! How sadly have you been abused by a faction [the rebel leaders] void of truth and void of tenderness to you and your country? . . . The spirit of the whole nation [of England] is in full activity against you. . . . All orders and ranks of men in Great Britain are now unanimous and determined to risk their all in the contest. . . . In a word, your harbors are blocked up, your cities [will] fall one after another, fortress after fortress, battle after battle, [will be] lost."

patriots as traitors, spied on them, and even openly took up arms against them. (Nearly fifty thousand Loyalists fought in the British ranks during the conflict.) This made the American Revolution not only a war for independence, but also a civil war in which neighbor fought neighbor.

INITIAL AMERICAN LOSSES

The first major battle fought following the publication of the Declaration of Independence clearly demonstrated British superiority in numbers, arms, organization, and training. In August 1776, General William Howe approached New York City, then the second largest city in America after Philadelphia. His goals were to establish a strong British base of operations and to drive a wedge between the New England states and southern states. Washington attempted to stop Howe but lacked sufficient manpower

and weapons to do so. "Badly beaten at Brooklyn Heights on August 27, 1776," historian Richard Hofstadter writes,

> Washington ferried his mauled army across the East River. . . . He retreated again from Harlem Heights to White Plains and thence across the Hudson to New Jersey. . . . Had General Howe pursued the retreating patriot army or if he had invaded New England in November 1776, he might have crushed colonial resistance. But instead, he . . . moved his army into winter quarters. Washington retreated into Pennsylvania as winter and gloom descended over his ragged Continentals.[73]

Following these initial losses, Washington and other American leaders took stock of their precarious predicament. Not only was the Continental army smaller and less well trained than its

British counterpart, but the Americans had few experienced officers. Also, Washington pointed out, the term of service for ordinary soldiers was too short. No sooner did the average Continental regular complete his training, when his hitch was over and he returned to civilian life. "Good God!" Washington bellowed at a group of congressmen visiting his Pennsylvania military camp. "Our cause is ruined if you engage men for only a year. If we ever hope for success, we must have men enlisted for the whole term of the war!"[74] (Luckily for the American war effort, Congress heeded Washington's call and increased the term of service to three years.)

General William Howe is sometimes blamed for the loss of the Revolutionary War.

WASHINGTON'S CHRISTMAS SURPRISE

Despite their many military disadvantages, the Americans did have one factor working in their favor, namely, the arrogance and overconfidence of many of the British commanders. General Howe's failure to follow up on his victory in New York was a typical example. Howe believed that he could defeat Washington's small, inexperienced army at any given place and time. And in his conceit, the British commander settled down for the winter with his troops, half of whom were German mercenaries.

Howe also did nothing to prevent the Germans from rampaging through New Jersey villages and countryside. They "looted the houses of Loyalists and rebels indiscriminately," Thomas Fleming writes. "Not a few supporters of George III changed their minds after their homes were stripped of valuables. Even feather beds were stolen."[75] A large force of Germans also occupied the town of Trenton, on the Delaware River, placing them within striking distance of the U.S. capital —Philadelphia.

George Washington watched these developments warily. He realized that he must achieve a victory soon; otherwise, the American cause might be lost. That would mean that "America would never pursue a separate destiny," as Fleming puts it. The Americans would have no choice but to "accept what Howe offered —British liberty, carefully circumscribed by the king and his nobles. Americans would be meek, humble, second-class citizens of the omnipotent empire."[76]

In desperation, Washington organized a bold plan for a surprise attack. On

General Washington, commander of the Continental Army, leads his troops across the Delaware River. Their subsequent surprise attack on Britian's German allies ended in decisive victory.

Christmas Day, 1776, he led twenty-four hundred troops across the Delaware in the middle of the night. "For landing craft," Samuel Morison tells it,

Washington had a fleet of Durham boats, 30 to 40 feet long, whose peacetime employment was to carry freight on the Delaware. Each was manned by four or five men. . . . The crossing started at 7:00 P.M. By 3:00 A.M. all the men and 18 fieldpieces [cannons] were across. It took an hour to form the regiments on the east bank. At 4:00 December 26, the advance began in two columns through the snow and in a biting wind. Sunrise found the columns a mile from Trenton, where [the Germans] were sleeping off Christmas. They were completely surprised, their retreat cut off, and . . . the German officers decided to surrender. At the cost of none killed, four wounded, but two frozen to death, Washington captured over 900 prisoners, 1,200 small arms, [and] 6 brass cannons.[77]

FACING A COUNTRYSIDE IN ARMS

When the news of Washington's triumph over the German mercenaries at Trenton spread, the American cause received a needed boost of support. Enlistments in the Continental army suddenly increased; and militiamen from Pennsylvania and other states swarmed to the aid of Washington's bedraggled but victorious regulars. Encouraged by the sudden change of fortune, the Americans scored another victory, only a week after the Trenton win, this time at Princeton, New Jersey.

The Americans enjoyed still another important win later in 1777 when British general John Burgoyne marched an army southward from Canada in an effort to conquer northern New York and the New England states. Like Howe, Burgoyne was arrogant and thought his formidable forces could easily overcome any local resistance. However, on the march Burgoyne soon encountered a phenomenon for which he, as well as other British leaders, was ill prepared. Seemingly out of nowhere, groups of local patriots harassed and attacked his supply trains and fired on his columns, spreading confusion and fear.

This tactic was effective against the British because they had never before encountered a whole countryside of angry, armed people. Back in Europe, an army on the march could expect to move safely through the countryside until it met up with enemy troops and engaged in a pitched battle. The frightened local townspeople and peasants almost always laid low or ran away. In America, by contrast, as Burgoyne himself later recalled:

Wherever the King's forces point, militia, to the number of three or four thousand, assemble in twenty-four hours. They bring with them their subsistence [food and other supplies], etc., and, the alarm over, they return to their farms. The Hampshire Grants [what is now Vermont] in particular . . . hangs like a gathering storm upon my left. In all parts [of the countryside] the [rebels'] industry and management in driving cattle and removing corn are indefatigable [untiring].[78]

Burgoyne lost so many men, by a combination of death, wounding, and desertion, that he finally admitted defeat. He surrendered to American general Horatio Gates on October 17, 1777.

THE NAVAL WAR

Though the Americans had racked up some impressive victories, they had to face the reality that, so far, Britain had committed only a small fraction of its potential armed might to the war effort in America. Britain could easily commit more troops. And the British still controlled most of America's coastal waters. American leaders realized that they could not win the war unless they could somehow match or at least neutralize British sea power.

The infant American navy cannot be faulted for lack of effort in this respect. If American warships could not match British warships in raw tonnage and firepower, the thinking went, perhaps they could outmaneuver the British navy. For example, Patriot leader Robert Morris urged American naval officer John Paul Jones to draw British vessels away from U.S. cities by attacking the British in the

West Indies and Florida. In Morris's view, "Destroying their settlements, spreading alarms, showing and keeping up a spirit of enterprise" would "oblige them to defend their extensive possessions at all points. If they divide their force, we shall have elbow room and, that gained, we shall turn about and play our parts to the best advantage."[79]

Jones not only followed this advice, he also carried the naval war to Britain's own shores. In a series of bold raids on

THE BATTLE ON LAKE CHAMPLAIN

This is part of Benedict Arnold's own recollection (quoted in volume 1 of Henry Commager and Richard Morris's Spirit of 'Seventy-Six) *of the battle fought on Lake Champlain in October 1776.*

"Yesterday morning at eight o'clock, the enemy's fleet, consisting of [two ships] mounting sixteen guns . . . one schooner of fourteen guns, two of twelve, [and other vessels] . . . appeared off Cumberland Head. We immediately prepared to receive them. . . . At eleven o'clock they . . . began the attack. The schooner, by some bad management, fell to leeward and was first attacked; one of her masts was wounded, and her rigging shot away. The captain thought prudent to run her [aground]. . . . They boarded her, and at night set fire to her. At half-past twelve the engagement became general and very warm [intense]. Some of the enemy's ships . . . beat and rowed up within musket-shot of us. They continued a very hot fire with round and grape-shot until five o'clock, when they thought proper to retire to about six or seven hundred yards distance, and continued the fire until dark. The [American vessels] *Congress* and *Washington* have suffered greatly. . . . The *New York* lost all her officers, except her captain. The *Philadelphia* was hulled [poked with holes] in so many places that she sunk in about one hour after the engagement was over. The whole [number of Americans] killed and wounded amounts to about sixty."

English and Irish coasts beginning in April 1778, he captured a small British warship, the *Drake*; and the following year, he defeated the larger British warship *Serapis*, which boasted forty-four cannons.

Meanwhile, back in North America, British and American ships clashed on Lake Champlain. In October 1776, a small American naval squadron commanded by Benedict Arnold (who would later defect to the British) attacked a larger British force in hopes of delaying an enemy invasion of New York and New England. Arnold ultimately lost the battle. However, he cost the British much time, energy, and supplies, which forced them to put off and eventually to cancel their invasion. In the words of noted nineteenth-century naval historian Alfred T. Mahan, "Never had any force, big or small, lived to better purpose, or died more gloriously. . . . [Later crucial American victories were] due to the invaluable year of delay secured to them by their little navy on Lake Champlain."[80]

A considerably bigger positive development seemed to materialize in the naval war when, in February 1778, the United States signed a treaty of alliance with France. The French possessed a navy almost as strong as Britain's. Hoping to hinder the British, their traditional enemies, the French pledged to fight alongside the Americans until Britain acknowledged the state of independence declared in the recent Declaration.

Unfortunately for the American war effort, however, the French were very slow in mounting an offensive. It was not until 1779 that they dispatched a fleet of warships to aid the United States; and this fleet, commanded by the Comte d'Es-

taing, was badly damaged in a fight with British warships near Tybee Island, in Georgia. Collecting his remaining vessels, d'Estaing returned to France. The French promised to send another fleet, but there was no way of knowing when this would happen. Thus, Washington and other patriot leaders now realized, America would have to continue to face the British alone for at least several months and possibly longer.

TERROR AND REVENGE IN THE SOUTH

During the period of a year and a half that followed d'Estaing's withdrawal, most of the fighting in the conflict occurred in North and South Carolina. This combat proved to be both bloody and tragic. Soldiers from both sides assaulted civilians and destroyed a great deal of property in an effort to terrorize the enemy, acts clearly contrary to the high humanitarian ideals expressed by Jefferson in the Declaration of Independence. Indeed, the once-peaceful and picturesque countryside in the Carolinas and Georgia became a nightmarish landscape; neighbor frequently fought neighbor, and bloody revenge raids in which whole families were slaughtered were common.

Some local American militia groups joined this free-for-all by forming guerrilla bands that raided British camps and supply lines and terrorized leading Loyalists. One of the more famous of these guerrilla leaders was Francis Marion, a former officer in the Continental army. He and his men were intimately familiar with the backwoods and swamps of South Carolina and usually retreated to these areas after their raids. For this reason, Marion became known as the "Swamp Fox." (The rebel leader played by Mel Gibson in the 2000 film *The Patriot* was loosely based on Marion.)

The British naturally wanted to catch rebels like Marion and cited brutal American tactics to justify the numerous atrocities perpetrated by British soldiers and local Loyalists. The British effort in the Carolinas was led by Lord Charles Cornwallis. He captured Charleston, South Carolina, in May 1780 and followed it up with a ruthless attack on nearby villages and farms. He instituted a harsh policy that dictated that any person who refused to aid and support the British would be imprisoned and have his or her property confiscated. Further, any American who joined a rebel militia or guerrilla group and got caught would be subject to immediate execution without trial. In one incident, the Loyalist in charge of Augusta, Georgia, found about twenty seriously wounded patriots who had taken part in a raid on the town; he pitilessly hung thirteen of them in the stairwell of his own house.

In another case, a seventeen-year-old patriot named James Collins witnessed a raid by British and Loyalists in which "women were insulted and stripped of every article of decent clothing they might have on." The Loyalists, Collins said, "even entered houses where men were sick of the smallpox . . . dragged them out of their sickbeds into the yard and put them to death in cold blood in the presence of their wives and children."[81]

Known as the "Swamp Fox," Francis Marion and his guerrilla fighters made many daring raids on British encampments throughout much of South Carolina.

Victory at Cowpens

The only hope of survival, much less victory, for the patriots living in the Carolinas and Georgia was the intervention of a capable army commander who could organize U.S. forces in the region into a coherent fighting force. This finally took place late in 1780. Congress urged General Washington to choose such an officer. And he gave command of patriot forces in the South to Nathanael Greene, a gifted thirty-eight-year-old from Rhode Island. In an amazingly short span of time, Greene whipped a weary, badly supplied group of regulars and militiamen into fighting shape. He also divided his forces into two sections, with himself in charge of one and another capable officer, Daniel Morgan, in command of the other.

On January 17, 1781, Morgan encountered a British force at Cowpens, near the border between the two Carolinas. Preparing for battle, the British commander, cavalry leader Colonel Banastre Tarleton, placed his infantry in the middle and cavalry units on his wings. Morgan ordered his own troops to form three lines. His militiamen stood in front, then came his regulars, and his horsemen took up the rear. Tarleton ordered a bayonet charge against the American ranks. But Morgan was prepared with a surprise maneuver. His men suddenly pulled back, as if retreating, and the British regulars, now overconfident and sensing victory, charged forward wildly. This caused the British ranks to become disorganized, at which point Morgan's troops stopped, turned, and fired on the onrushing enemy at nearly point-blank range. Then the American regulars launched their own bayonet charge, which smashed the British lines.

Of his 1,100 men, Tarleton lost 100 killed, 200 wounded, and more than 600 captured. Morgan lost only 12 killed and 60 wounded.

Following the American victory at Cowpens, Greene and Morgan continued to inflict heavy losses on the British. Eventually, Greene managed to drive the enemy back to Charleston. Now convinced that he could not defeat the Americans in the Carolinas, Cornwallis opted to try to achieve victory in Virginia. He moved northward and set up his new headquarters at Yorktown, facing Chesapeake Bay in southern Virginia.

The World Turned Upside Down

Cornwallis's occupation of Yorktown turned out to be a fatal mistake. Even as the British were settling in, the new fleet the French had promised so many months before was at last bearing down on the Virginia coast. When General Washington heard the news, he could barely contain his joy. According to an eyewitness, the tall Virginian's normally austere demeanor temporarily melted away and he "acted like a child whose every wish has been gratified [fulfilled]."[82]

Cornwallis and his forces were now trapped in Yorktown. Washington's army blocked the escape route on the city's land side, while the French fleet covered Yorktown's seaward flank. On September 28, 1781, the American and French allied forces opened fire on Yorktown from both sides. At first, Cornwallis attempted to dig himself in and resist. But the allied artillery barrage was so immense and frightening that it soon became clear that the British position was hopeless. On October 19, Cornwallis did what most British leaders viewed as impossible, even unthinkable—he surrendered.

Cornwallis sent his second in command, General Charles O'Hara, to the formal surrender ceremony. There, General Benjamin Lincoln, standing in for George Washington, accepted the British commander's sword. Meanwhile, the defeated British troops filed out of the city. As Samuel Morison tells it:

> One by one, the British regiments, after laying down their arms, marched back to camp between two lines, one of American soldiers, the other of French, while the military bands played a series of melancholy tunes, including one which all recognized as "The World Turned Upside Down."[83]

In two ways, the world *had* been turned upside down. First, the American victory at Yorktown proved to be the decisive event of the war. The British no longer had the stomach to continue a major struggle so far from home, especially with their mounting losses and the increasing strength and sheer tenacity of the American rebels. Thus, although no official peace treaty had yet been signed, nearly everyone realized that the war was over. A small ragtag group of rebellious colonists had defeated the most powerful empire on Earth.

The peace treaty officially acknowledging the American victory took nearly two years to negotiate. There were many serious issues on which it was difficult to find agreement, including the new nation's recognized boundaries, fishing rights in coastal waters, and restoration of property and civil rights to former British Loyalists in America. France also had issues it wanted addressed,

MAJOR BATTLES OF THE REVOLUTIONARY WAR

Quebec
Dec. 31, 1775

Nova Scotia

Montreal
Nov. 13, 1775

Maine
(Part of Mass.)

Crown Point

Ft. Ticonderoga

New Hampshire

Saratoga
Oct. 17, 1777

Concord (Apr. 19, 1775)
Lexington (Apr. 19, 1775)
Bunker Hill (June 17, 1775)

L. Ontario

Oriskany
Aug. 6, 1777

Bennington
Aug. 16, 1777

Massachusetts

New York

Rhode Island
Connecticut

L. Erie

White Plains

Pennsylvania

Long Island (Aug. 27, 1776)
Princeton (Jan. 3, 1777)
Monmouth (June 28, 1778)
Trenton (Dec. 26, 1776)

Germantown
Oct. 4, 1777

Brandywine
Sep. 11, 1777

New Jersey

Delaware

Maryland

Virginia

ATLANTIC OCEAN

Yorktown
Oct. 6-19, 1781

Great Bridge
Dec. 9, 1775

Guilford Courthouse
March 15, 1781

Kings Mountain
Oct. 7, 1780

North Carolina

Cowpens
Jan. 17, 1781

Moore's Creek Bridge
Feb. 27, 1776

Camden
Aug. 16, 1780

South Carolina

Charleston
May 12, 1780

Georgia

Savannah
Dec. 29, 1778

The Artillery Barrage at Yorktown

An American surgeon, James Thatcher, witnessed the huge American and French artillery barrage at Yorktown. This is part of the account he penned in his military journal.

"From the 10th to the 15th, a tremendous and incessant firing from the American and French batteries is kept up, and the enemy returned the fire, but with little effect. A red-hot shell from the French battery set fire to the *Charon*, a British 44-gun ship, and two or three smaller vessels at anchor in the river, which were consumed in the night. From the banks of the river, I had a fine view of this splendid conflagration. The ships were enwrapped in a torrent of fire, which spread with vivid brightness among the combustible rigging . . . while all around was thunder and lightning from our numerous cannon and mortars, and in the darkness of the night, presented one of the most sublime and magnificent spectacles which can be imagined. Some of our shells, overreaching the town, are seen to fall into the river, and bursting, throw up columns of water like shooting of the monsters of the deep."

which made the negotiations drag on and on. Finally, on September 3, 1783, the parties signed the Treaty of Paris (so named because the negotiations took place in that French city). America's war for independence was at last officially over.

The second way that the world had been turned upside down was more long term in nature and not something that most people then living could have clearly foreseen. The victory attained by the American patriots against incredible odds had set an example for other peoples who yearned for freedom and self-rule. And in the years that followed, the old European order of kings and empires steadily began to crumble. Moreover, the Declaration of Independence, far from being trampled under British boots, survived and became a cherished symbol of freedom. The daring, heart-stirring phrases emblazoned in the document came to inspire countless people in all corners of the globe, who saw from the American example that freedom and democracy were possible and well worth fighting for.

6 The Declaration Inspires a Larger Revolution

In the decades and centuries following the American Revolution, the Declaration of Independence became renowned the world over and came to influence and inspire millions of people. "No other American document has been read so often or listened to by so many weary and perspiring audiences," respected Jefferson biographer Dumas Malone writes. "Yet, despite interminable repetition, those well-worn phrases have never lost their potency and charm."[84]

This turn of events is not surprising. The document turned out to be much more than a mere statement of American independence relevant primarily to the 1770s. In their zeal for justice, freedom, and independence, the American founders stated profound moral truths that are potentially applicable to all peoples and nations in all ages. This can be seen clearly in Jefferson's opening words: "When in the course of human events." It was in the framework of "human" events, not merely "American" or "English-speaking" events, that he placed the American struggle. Similarly, the words of the Declaration went beyond British and American laws and invoked the "laws of Nature and of Nature's God." As noted American historian Henry S. Commager points out, "No other political document of the eighteenth century proclaimed so broad a purpose; no political document of our own

day associates the United States so boldly with universal history and the cosmic system."[85]

In addition to stating in dramatic terms several universally recognized human rights and laws, the Declaration also became the world's most elegant and compelling rationale for the creation of democratic government. In phrases such as "all men are created equal," "unalienable rights," and "governments . . . deriving their just powers from the consent of the governed," the Declaration implied that democracy is not only desirable, but also the best and fairest system available to human beings. Either directly or indirectly, Jefferson and his colleagues advocated that the ultimate end of government must be the happiness of its citizens; and such happiness can only be fully achieved by open democracy. Adopting such a stance in 1776 was both extremely radical and audacious. After all, at the time no other true democracy existed on Earth (although Britain was at least partially democratic).

Despite the boldness of their stirring statement of independence, most of the founders did not then foresee that they were setting in motion a process of worldwide democratization. There was no guarantee that the fledgling American democracy would long survive in a world filled with absolute monarchies and empires.

Certainly, few people then living could have imagined that democracy would sweep across the world in the centuries to come. On this point, once again Thomas Jefferson proved the most visionary of the founders. In a letter penned in June 1826, shortly before his death, he captured a glimpse of a future world shaped in part by the principles of the timeless document he had written:

The Declaration of Independence is renowned throughout the world as an eloquent articulation of democratic principles, as well as profound moral truths.

TO BURST THE CHAINS OF IGNORANCE

This letter written by Thomas Jefferson on June 24, 1826 (quoted in Merrill D. Peterson's compilation of Jefferson's writings), is a response to an invitation to attend the fiftieth anniversary celebration of the Declaration of Independence.

"The kind invitation I receive from you, on the part of the citizens of Washington, to be present with them at their celebration on the fiftieth anniversary of American Independence, as one of the surviving signers of [the Declaration] . . . is most flattering. . . . [Though I cannot attend, I would have delighted in meeting with the other surviving founding fathers]. . . . May it [the Declaration] be to the world, what I believe it will be (to some parts sooner, to others later, but finally to all), the signal of arousing men to burst the chains under which monkish ignorance and superstition had persuaded them to bind themselves, and to assume the blessings and security of self-government. That form which we have substituted, restores the free right to the unbounded exercise of reason and freedom of opinion. All eyes are opened, or opening, to the rights of man. The general spread of the light of science has already laid open to every view the palpable truth, that the mass of mankind has not been born with saddles on their backs, nor a favored few booted and spurred, ready to ride them. . . . These are grounds of hope for others. For ourselves, let the annual return of this day forever refresh our recollections of these rights, and an undiminished devotion to them."

May it [the Declaration] be to the world, what I believe it will be (to some parts sooner, to others later, but finally to all), the signal of arousing men to burst the chains under which monkish ignorance and superstition had persuaded them to bind themselves, and to assume the blessings and security of self-government. . . . All eyes are opened, or opening, to the rights of man. . . . The mass of mankind has not been born with saddles on their backs, nor a favored few . . . [born] ready to ride them. . . . These are grounds of hope for others.[86]

JOURNEYS OF A PARCHMENT AND ITS IDEALS

The following summary of the life and influence of the Declaration of Independence shows how Jefferson's vision of the

The Declaration is housed in the exhibition hall of the National Archives in Washington, D.C.

future did come to pass (at least partially, for even today the global democratic revolution remains far from complete). During the first 176 years of its existence, the original parchment copy of the Declaration had no permanent home. It traveled far and wide as public officials in various states and cities vied for the opportunity to put it on display. In this period, the document twice narrowly escaped destruction by fire. Also, the British nearly captured it during both the Revolutionary War and the War of 1812.

Over time, this original copy of the Declaration became sadly worse for wear. Its ink had dimmed considerably due to the effects of bright light, and some of the historic signatures had been damaged by repeated rolling and unrolling of the parchment. In 1894, therefore, some public officials in Washington, D.C., consigned the document to a metal safe in the library of the U.S. Department of State. The Declaration remained there until 1921, at which time other officials moved it to the Library of Congress. Finally, in 1952, the document was placed permanently in a display case in the exhibition hall of the National Archives in Washington, D.C.

This was the fate of what largely amounts to a piece of paper, although certainly one viewed as a precious relic. The democratic ideals inscribed on that piece of paper are the real substance of the Declaration, and these were destined for a much longer journey than the venerable old parchment. Following the American victory over Britain in the early 1780s, people in many foreign lands read copies of the Declaration and watched the infant United States with great interest. Large numbers of these distant observers had little hope that the new country could survive very long in a world dominated by powerful monarchies.

Yet these doubts proved premature. The American experiment continued to unfold, as the United States won wars and overcame other serious crises in decade after decade. The new nation demonstrated that a government ruled by the people could not only survive, but prosper and grow. Indeed, over the years the United States grew steadily larger and militarily stronger. Meanwhile, its political institutions kept pace, becoming increasingly more democratic and allowing more and more minorities and other groups a chance to share in the American dream.

People around the world saw these positive results of the American experiment and began to react in one of two ways. Some decided that their best chance to exercise the right to happiness, which Jefferson cited as a primary human birthright in the Declaration, was to become Americans themselves. In the nineteenth and early twentieth centuries, therefore, huge numbers of people from Europe, Asia, and elsewhere immigrated to the United States. Even more foreigners reacted to the successful American experiment in a different way. Inspired by the principles of the Declaration of Independence and the U.S. Constitution (framed in 1789), they launched various revolutions of their own in an effort to be free and independent in their own right.

LIBERTY AWAKENS IN FRANCE

The first people thus inspired by the Declaration's liberal principles were the French, whose aid during the American Revolution had been instrumental in the ultimate victory. While the British and Americans were at war in the 1770s and 1780s, France was fast approaching the brink of serious economic and social disaster. Recent French monarchs, especially Louis XV (who reigned from 1715 to 1774) and Louis XVI (1774–1792), had been arrogant, wasteful, and their regimes repressive. The French people grew increasingly restless, unhappy, and ripe for revolt.

Considering this situation, it is not surprising that many French citizens were fascinated with and inspired by the American Revolution and its democratic ideals. The American war for independence "seems first to have awakened the thinking part of the French nation in general from the sleep of despotism in which they were sunk," Jefferson later recalled in his autobiography.

> The [French] officers too, who had been to America, were mostly young men, less shackled by habit and prejudice, and more ready to assent to the suggestions of common sense, and feeling of common rights, than others. They came back with new ideas and impressions.[87]

One Frenchwoman who was duly impressed with the Americans and felt strong sympathy for and solidarity with them and their cause was the Vicomtesse de Fars-Fausselandry. "The American cause seemed to be our own," she later wrote.

The American Example

Although the American Revolution did not directly incite the French Revolution, it demonstrated to France that such a fight could actually be won by people with a just cause. The Marquis de Condorcet, an Enlightenment philosopher, made this statement (quoted in Carl Becker's book on the Declaration):

"It is not enough that human rights should be written in the books of philosophers and in the hearts of virtuous men; it is necessary that ignorant or weak men should read them in the example of a great people. America has given us this example. The act which declares its independence is a simple and sublime exposition of those rights so sacred and so long forgotten."

We were proud of their victories, we cried at their defeats, we tore down [news] bulletins [posted on buildings and lampposts] and read them in all our houses. None of us reflected on the danger the New World could give to the old [by inspiring Europeans to rise up against their own governments].[88]

Yet this constant barrage of news about the fight for freedom in America *did* prove dangerous, at least to the French crown and nobles. According to Jefferson, who was in Paris serving as U.S. ambassador to France in the period just preceding the outbreak of the French Revolution:

The [French] press, notwithstanding its shackles, began to disseminate them [facts about the war]; conversation assumed new freedoms; politics became the theme of all societies [social circles], male and female, and a very extensive and zealous party was formed, which acquired the appellation of the Patriotic party, who, sensible of the abusive government under which they had lived, sighed for occasions of reforming it.[89]

Many of the people who made up this French patriotic party felt that the new American democratic system should and would be imitated by other nations. One liberal writer, Abbé Gentil, was particularly forward-looking and optimistic for his day. "It is in the heart of this newborn republic," he said of the United States, "that the true treasures that will enrich the world will lie."[90] Another liberal French thinker and writer, Abbé Robin, liked the idea that Americans seemed to care far less about class distinctions than the French and other Europeans. When an American army made camp, he pointed out, officers and ordinary soldiers, as well as men and women, all sang and danced together. "These people," Robin wrote, "are still in the happy time when distinctions of birth and rank are ignored and can see, with the same eye, the common soldier and the officer."[91]

Impressed by American equality before the French Revolution, the French patriots also drew inspiration from America once the Revolution had begun in 1789. The patriots admired Jefferson's Declaration of Independence and felt that they, too, needed such a document stating basic human rights and democratic ideals. The Marquis de Lafayette, an army officer who had fought alongside George Washington in the American Revolution, was the first Frenchman to propose a declaration of rights for his own country. In the summer of 1789, Lafayette penned several drafts and asked Jefferson, who was still in Paris, to read and comment on them. Happy to oblige, Jefferson made several additions that Lafayette heartily approved of.

EVENTS LEADING TO THE FRENCH DECLARATION

It was not Lafayette's version of the French declaration that the French patriots finally adopted, however. Some members of the Assembly, a new legislature that claimed to be France's rightful government, issued their own version on August 27, 1789. The now world-famous document, titled the Declaration of the Rights of Man and of the Citizen, is more radical than the American Declaration. The French Declaration also features a different format than its American counterpart. Instead of a syllogism, the format chosen by Jefferson, the French version consists of a list of basic rights; so in many ways it resembles the American Bill of Rights (ratified in 1791).

That the French Declaration ended up looking like a bill of rights is not surprising. Before the outbreak of violence and drafting of the Declaration, the French patriots did not desire or intend to eliminate the monarchy and establish a democracy in its place. Rather, they simply hoped to draft written guarantees that all French citizens, regardless of social class, would enjoy basic civil rights, and then to have the king agree to these guarantees. That would make France a constitutional monarchy (like Britain), in which the king's authority rested on the will of the people and their legislative representatives.

Had the king and his aristocratic supporters made this reasonable concession, they probably would have retained their high positions and a violent revolution would have been avoided. However, the king badly mishandled the situation. In large degree, this was because he was unduly influenced by members of the royal family and a few disgruntled conservative aristocrats, all of whom were terrified of losing their huge power and wealth. In the early summer of 1789, the king ordered troops to begin massing in the outskirts of Versailles (the location of his palace) and Paris. This move caused extreme anxiety in the streets of the capital. Worried that the troops might enter the city and attack the patriotic Assembly, many people in Paris and neighboring towns began collecting arms.

On July 14, the search for weapons led a large crowd to march to the Bastille, the fortress-prison in which the government had once kept its political prisoners. This facility had come to be seen as a hated symbol of the monarchy's many abuses of the people. Unfortunately, the governor of the fortress, out of fear and ineptitude, ordered his guards to fire on the crowd; ninety-eight people were killed and many others wounded. Hundreds of the angry survivors then captured the fortress and executed the governor and several of his men. Ever since, July 14 has been called "Bastille Day" and celebrated as France's independence day.

Following the Bastille's fall, similar uprisings and demonstrations against the government occurred in other parts of the country. Rumors spread that the king would order his troops into rural areas and suppress any dissent by the peasants. Swept along by what became known as the "Great Fear," many peasants burned rich mansions and destroyed other property. Moved by these demonstrations, in a dramatic gesture on the night of August 4, many aristocrats renounced their feudal rights. From that moment on, all French citizens were theoretically equal under the law. This preliminary establishment of equality paved the way for the patriots to draft their Declaration of the Rights of Man and of the Citizen on August 27.

DEMOCRACY SPREADS AROUND THE GLOBE

The American and French Revolutions turned out to be only the beginning of a larger worldwide democratic revolution. The democratic principles of the French Revolution, which had been partly inspired by those of the American version,

The fall of the Bastille on July 14, 1789, is celebrated today as the beginning of French independence.

directly inspired revolutionary activity in many other lands. "The French Revolution," historian J.L. Talmon points out,

> proclaimed the rights of man and promised equality. And from then onwards, not only [social] burdens and humiliations which had previously been borne [by the people] as an inescapable fate of the station of life . . . but [also] any injury to what came to be thought of as the dignity of man, began to appear as intolerable, and justifying resistance.[92]

The spread of insurrections and establishment of democracies did not happen all at once. In Europe, for example, the spirit of freedom and independence grew slowly but steadily beneath the seemingly normal surface of society all through the early 1800s. Finally, in 1848, a sort of revolutionary fervor erupted in many parts of Europe. The spark that touched off the explosion was a second French uprising (less violent than the 1789 version), in which the French people demanded universal voting rights and guarantees that the working classes would have ample jobs. The former government was swept away and France's Second Republic established.

The news of these events spread rapidly. And as scholar Melvin Kranzberg puts it in his book about the 1848 uprisings:

> The insurrection in Paris set off a revolutionary "chain reaction." Within a few weeks, revolutions had broken out in Vienna [Austria], Berlin [Germany], Milan [Italy], Budapest [Hungary]—indeed, in all the German and Italian states and throughout the Hapsburg domains [areas of Europe ruled by members of an old German dynasty]. In the spring of 1848, the revolutionary cause seemed successful everywhere. . . . The rulers of the German and Italian states, as well as the powerful Hapsburg emperor, were forced to grant liberal constitutions to their subjects. Even more striking was the fact that the Italians seemed well on their way to achieving national unity, while the German states sent representatives to a National Assembly in Frankfurt, where the constitution for a unified Germany was to be worked out.[93]

Meanwhile, in Hungary, the people clamored for and received a new constitution that recognized several basic human rights. Unfortunately, within three years, the momentum of this liberal political movement had slowed; and none of these countries instituted full democracy at this time. Still, the 1848 revolutions were a crucial step in Europe's march toward democracy. They firmly implanted the ideals of liberty, social equality, and popular government in European soil. And over the course of the century that followed, nearly all European nations became democracies.

The influence of the American Revolution and the Declaration of Independence on these events was indirect, mostly funneled through the French revolutionary experience. By comparison, the influence of American democracy was a good deal more direct in South America, the Pacific region, and Asia. For example, in 1810 local patriots in Venezuela launched an insurrection aimed at gaining independence from their colonial

Inspired by the ideals of Jefferson's Declaration, Venezuelan patriots fought to gain their nation's independence from Spain. Here, Simon Bolivar and Francisco de Miranda sign Venezuela's Declaration of Independence.

master, Spain. Francisco de Miranda, one of the leading Venezuelan patriots, had fought in both the American and French Revolutions and was especially impressed by the liberal democratic ideals expressed by Jefferson in the Declaration of Independence. Driven by these ideals, Venezuela's revolutionary congress declared the nation's independence from Spain on July 5, 1811; and the revolutionaries finally defeated and drove out the Spanish in 1821. (Sadly, Miranda was unjustly accused of betraying his comrades, who handed him over to the Spanish; he died in a Spanish prison in 1816.)

Liberal American ideals also strongly influenced the founding of democratic governments in Argentina (in 1816), Liberia (in western Africa, in 1847), the Philippines (in the South Pacific, in 1946), and a number of Central American na-

tions. Even when the end result was *not* liberal democracy, American influence played a key role. When Vietnam's revolutionary leader, Ho Chi Minh, proclaimed his land's independence in 1945, for instance, he modeled his own revolutionary declaration on the one written by Jefferson in 1776.

FREEDOM'S ECONOMIC FACTOR

The Philippines was not the only nation to feel the influence of the American Revolution and establish a democratic system in the twentieth century. In fact, that century witnessed the founding of a record number of democracies worldwide. By 1950, 22 nations had democratic governments, representing about 31 percent of the world's population. These numbers continued to increase; and by 2002, 120 of the world's 192 countries, representing roughly 63 percent of the world's people, had adopted full-blown democracy or at least some form of representative government. In at least three-quarters of these cases, the United States either inspired, sponsored, or otherwise helped to establish or nurture these governments.

This stupendous, thoroughly unprecedented reordering of world politics occurred partly because the United States became a military superpower in these years and used its authority and prestige to spread democracy around the globe. An even more crucial factor was the tremendous success of the market economy of the United States, especially in the years following World War II. Living standards rose sharply, greatly expanding the American middle class. And millions of people were able to own their own homes, buy two cars, and send their children to college.

Observers around the world saw that this economic success story had been accomplished largely through a spirit of free private enterprise and a strong market economy (capitalism). Through economic growth and security, therefore, the Americans had obtained much of the "happiness" that Jefferson and other Enlightenment thinkers had insisted was a central natural right of all human beings. As noted political scholars James Hoge and Fareed Zakaria point out, numerous other nations eventually saw the wisdom of imitating the American system, even if only its free markets:

Life at the end of the twentieth century [was] dominated by the idea and the reality of America's distinctive creed, liberal democratic capitalism. Nations and peoples of every culture [were] adapting their old world to these new ideas, and their countries [were] being revolutionized, slowly but surely, by it. Some of this transformation [was] the result of broad structural shifts like industrialization and modernization, but much of it [was] the result of one nation's efforts to stand for and fight for certain political and economic ideals. The American encounter [had] changed the world.[94]

THE AMERICAN CENTURY

Part of this "American encounter" has been a widespread acceptance of American values, many of which were stated clearly in the Declaration of Independence. This process was most pronounced in the twentieth century. According to former U.S. secretary of state Henry Kissinger, "In every century, there seems to emerge a country with the power, the will and the intellectual and moral impetus to shape the entire international system in accordance with its own values."[95] For example, the course of world events in the sixteenth century was largely shaped by Spain, which sent explorers to the New World and built a lucrative overseas empire. In the seventeenth century, France became an economic and political powerhouse and dictated a lion's share of the course of human events. Likewise, Britain and its huge wealth-producing overseas empire dominated the nineteenth century.

Finally, the major events and trends of the twentieth century were, unarguably, guided mostly by the United States, its needs, its deeds, and its interests. The Americans enjoyed enormous economic success, which others desired to imitate or share in; so the United States was able to export abroad many of the democratic ideas mentioned in the Declaration of Independence.

This exportation of American ideals was accomplished partly by including them in important international documents. The most famous example is the charter of the United Nations, which features a declaration of rights based to a large extent on the Declaration of Independence and the U.S. Bill of Rights. (The UN doc-

---

MAKING "DEMOCRACY SAFE FOR THE WORLD"

In this excerpt from his article "The Rise of Illiberal Democracy," noted political writer Fareed Zakaria warns that having elections and some democratic institutions is not enough. The people must constantly be sure to maintain liberty and the rule of law; otherwise democracy becomes weak and meaningless.

"Of course cultures vary, and different societies will require different frameworks of government. This is not a plea for the wholesale adoption of the American way but rather for a more [varied] conception of liberal democracy, one that emphasizes both parts of that phrase. Before new policies can be adopted, there lies an intellectual task of recovering the constitutional liberal tradition, central to the Western experience and to the development of good government throughout the world. Political progress in Western history has been the result of a growing recognition over the centuries that, as the Declaration of Independence puts it, human beings have 'certain inalienable rights' and that 'it is to secure these rights that governments are instituted.' If a democracy does not preserve liberty and law, that it is a democracy is a small consolation. Democracy without constitutional liberalism is not simply inadequate, but dangerous, bringing with it the erosion of liberty, the abuse of power, ethnic divisions, and even war. Eighty years ago, Woodrow Wilson took America into the twentieth century with a challenge, to make the world safe for democracy. As we approach the next century, our task is to make democracy safe for the world."

ument also contains elements of the French Declaration and English Bill of Rights.) "All human beings are born free and equal in dignity and rights," the UN declaration begins.

> They are endowed with reason and conscience and should act towards one another in a spirit of brotherhood. . . . Everyone is entitled to all the rights and freedoms set forth in this declaration, without distinction of any kind, such as race, color, sex, language, religion, political or other opinion, national or social origin, property, birth, or other status.[96]

Another section of the UN declaration sounds hauntingly like one of Jefferson's key statements in the American Declaration: "Everyone has the right to life, liberty, and security of person."[97] The only difference is the substitution of the words "security of person" for "the pursuit of happiness." Evidently, the framers of the UN document felt that a person has the potential to be "happy" if he or she is guaranteed life, freedom, and safety. Other rights listed in the UN declaration include

> Everyone has the right to recognition everywhere as a person before the law. . . . Everyone has the right to own property alone as well as in association with others. . . . Everyone has the right to freedom of opinion and expression. . . . Everyone has the right to take part in the Government of his country, directly or through freely chosen representatives. Everyone has the right to freely participate in the cultural life of the community, to

Democratic societies worldwide have incorporated the ideals of Jefferson's Declaration.

enjoy the arts, and to share in scientific advancement and its benefits.[98]

AMERICA'S SECOND REVOLUTION

In addition to the widespread global influence of the ideals of the Declaration of Independence in the past two centuries, these values transformed the United States itself in the same period. Over the years, the country has grown freer; in particular, various individual groups within American society have gained recognition and a political voice. In fact, one of the driving forces of American domestic history has been an ongoing social revolution no less important than the military revolution that gave birth to the nation. That social revolution has witnessed the gradual application of the principles of Jefferson's Declaration to groups that long lacked full civil rights.

Indeed, the immediate beneficiaries of America's initial military revolution were well-to-do white males like Jefferson, Washington, and the other founders.

In the wake of that insurrection, the United States enjoyed freedom from Britain and a new democratic government. However, society itself remained largely unchanged. Men who owned no property still had little or no political voice; women remained second-class citizens who could not vote; and blacks were still slaves whom the law regarded as only partially human. The Declaration of Independence had stated categorically that "all men are created equal, that they are endowed by their Creator with certain unalienable rights." Yet American society remained *un*equal, with the rights of large segments of the population clearly alienated.

Women's suffrage, or the right to vote, was a controversial issue in the early twentieth century. In 1920, the Nineteenth Amendment to the U.S. Constitution granted women that right.

All of this eventually changed, of course. The reality was that only the military aspect of the American Revolution ended in 1783, when Britain formally acknowledged American independence. The American social revolution was only just getting started. Jefferson and his fellows had created a bold new kind of government, one constructed on the *ideals* of equality and democratic opportunity for all. True, many of these ideals existed mainly on paper at first. But over time, increasing numbers of Americans of all walks of life came to see them as their birthright and demanded to benefit from them. Once set in motion, said the noted American historian J. Franklin Jameson in his now-classic statement of social revolution, the "stream of revolution" could not be stopped and it spread across the land. "Many economic desires, many social aspirations," he wrote,

> were set free by the political struggle, many aspects of colonial society profoundly altered by the forces thus let loose. The relations of social classes to one another, the institution of slavery, the system of land-holding, the course of business, the forms and spirit of the intellectual and religious life, all felt the transforming hand of revolution, all emerged from under it in shapes advanced many degrees nearer to those we know.[99]

Guided by the noble ideals enshrined by Jefferson in the Declaration of Independence, America's second revolution steadily and relentlessly reshaped American society. In each succeeding generation, group after group became in a sense new revolutionaries; they took Jefferson, Adams, Washington, and the other founders at their word, demanded their rights, and finally, often after long and difficult struggles, began to enjoy those rights. Among these groups were American blacks, who in the nineteenth century gained freedom and in the twentieth century social equality and civil rights; and women, who acquired the rights to vote and to work in jobs traditionally held by men. Sometimes in the courts, other times in the media, and occasionally in the streets, people fought for civil rights, justice, and fair treatment in accordance with the principles of the Declaration of Independence. Moreover, for some that fight is still ongoing. And even after all Americans have achieved equality, the same battle will continue to be waged in other lands. The enduring and powerful living legacy of the Declaration is that the struggle to transform its ideals into reality will never end until all people everywhere enjoy true and complete equality. Abraham Lincoln recognized this inspiring goal when he said that the American Revolution

> was not the mere matter of separation of the colonies from the motherland, but [of] that sentiment in the Declaration of Independence which gave liberty, not alone to the people of this country, but hope to all the world, for all future time. It was that which gave promise that in due time the weights would be lifted from the shoulders of all men, and that all should have an equal chance. This is the sentiment embodied in the Declaration of Independence.[100]

The Declaration of Independence

Excerpts from Original Documents Pertaining to the Declaration of Independence

Document 1: The Declaration of Independence

This is the final version of the document, accepted by the Continental Congress on July 4, 1776, after two days of debate and revision.

WHEN in the Course of human events, it becomes necessary for one people to dissolve the political bands which have connected them with another, and to assume among the Powers of the earth, the separate and equal Station to which the Laws of Nature and of Nature's God entitle them, a decent respect to the opinions of mankind requires that they should declare the causes which impel them to the separation.—We hold these truths to be self-evident, that all men are created equal, that they are endowed by their Creator with certain unalienable Rights, that among these are Life, Liberty, and the pursuit of Happiness.—That to secure these rights, Governments are instituted among Men, deriving their just powers from the consent of the governed. —That whenever any Form of Government becomes destructive of these ends, it is the Right of the People to alter or to abolish it, and to institute new Government, laying its foundation on such principles and organizing its powers in such form, as to them shall seem most likely to effect their Safety and Happiness. Prudence, indeed, will dictate that Governments long established should not be changed for light and transient causes; and accordingly all experience hath shewn, that mankind are more disposed to suffer, while evils are sufferable, than to right themselves by abolishing the forms to which they are accustomed. But when a long train of abuses and usurpations, pursuing invariably the same Object, evinces a design to reduce them under absolute Despotism, it is their right, it is their duty, to throw off such Government, and to provide new Guards for their future security.—Such has been the patient sufferance of these Colonies; and such is now the necessity which constrains them to alter their former System of Government. The history of the present King of Great Britain is a history of repeated injuries and usurpations, all having in direct object the establishment of an absolute Tyranny over these States. To prove this, let the Facts be submitted to a candid world.—He has refused his Assent to Laws, the most wholesome and necessary for the public good.—He has forbidden his Governors to pass Laws of immediate and pressing importance, unless suspended in their operation till his Assent should be obtained; and when so suspended, he has utterly neglected to attend to them.—He has refused to pass other Laws for the accommodation of large districts of people, unless those people would relinquish the right of Representation in the Legislature, a right inestimable to them and formidable to tyrants only.—He has called together legislative bodies at places unusual, uncomfortable, and distant from the depository of their public Records, for the sole purpose of fatiguing them into compliance with his measures.—He has dissolved Representative Houses repeatedly, for opposing with manly firmness his invasions on the rights of the people.—He has refused for a long time, after such dissolutions, to cause others to be elected; whereby the Legislative powers, incapable of Annihilation, have returned to the People at large for their exercise; the State remaining in the mean time exposed to all the dangers of invasion from without, and convulsions within.—He has endeavored to prevent the population of these States; for that purpose obstructing Laws for naturalization of Foreigners; refusing to pass others to encourage their migrations hither, and raising the conditions of new Appropriations of Lands. —He has obstructed the Administration of Justice, by refusing his Assent to Laws for establishing Judiciary Powers.—He has made Judges dependent on his Will alone, for the tenure of their offices, and the amount and payment of their salaries.—He has erected a multitude of New Offices, and sent hither swarms of Officers to harass our people, and eat out their substance.—He has kept among us, in times of peace, Standing Armies without the Consent of our Legislatures. —He has affected to render the Military independent of and superior to the Civil power.—He has combined with others to subject us to a jurisdiction foreign to our constitution, and unacknowledged by our laws; giving his Assent to their Acts of pretended Legislation:—For quartering large bodies of armed troops among us:—For protecting them by a mock Trial, from punishment for any Murders which they should commit on the Inhabitants of these States:—For cutting off our Trade with all parts of the World:—For imposing Taxes on us without our Consent:—For depriving us in many cases of the benefits of Trial by Jury:—For transporting us beyond Seas to be tried for pretended offenses:—For abolishing the free System of English Laws in a neighboring—Province, establishing therein all Arbitrary government, and enlarging its Boundaries so as to render it at once an example and fit instrument for introducing the same absolute rule into these Colonies:—For taking away our Charters, abolishing our most valuable Laws, and altering fundamentally the Forms of our Governments:—For suspending our own Legislatures, and declaring themselves invested with power to legislate for us in all cases whatsoever.—He has abdicated Government here, by declaring us out of his Protection and waging war against us.—He has plundered our seas, ravaged our Coasts, burnt our towns, and destroyed the lives of our people.—He is at this time transporting large Armies of Foreign Mercenaries to complete the works of death, desolation and tyranny, already begun with circumstances of Cruelty and perfidy scarcely paralleled in the most barbarous ages, and totally unworthy the Head of a civilized nation.—He has constrained our fellow Citizens taken captive on the high Seas to bear Arms against their Country, to become the executioners of their friends and Brethren, or to fall themselves by their Hands.—He has excited domestic insurrections amongst us, and has endeavored to bring on the inhabitants of our frontiers, the merciless Indian Savages, whose rule of warfare is an undistinguished destruction of all ages, sexes and conditions. In every stage of these Oppressions We have Petitioned for Redress in the most humble terms. Our repeated Petitions have been answered only by repeated injury. A Prince, whose character is thus Marked by every act which may define a Tyrant, is unfit to be the ruler of a free people.—Nor have We been wanting in attentions to our British brethren. We have warned them from time to time of attempts by their legislature to extend an unwarrantable jurisdiction over us. We have reminded them of the circumstances of our emigration and settlement here. We have appealed to their native justice and magnanimity, and we have conjured them by the ties of our common kindred to disavow these usurpations, which would inevitably interrupt our connections and correspondence. They too have been deaf to the voice of justice and of consanguinity. We must, therefore, acquiesce in the necessity which denounces our Separation, and hold them, as we hold the rest of mankind. Enemies in War, in Peace Friends.

WE THEREFORE, the Representatives of the UNITED STATES OF AMERICA, in General Congress, Assembled, appealing to the Supreme Judge of the world for the rectitude of our intentions, do, in the Name, and by the authority of the good People of these Colonies, solemnly publish and declare, That these United Colonies are and of Right ought to be Free and Independent States: that they are Absolved from all Allegiance to the British Crown, and that all political connection between them and the State of Great Britain, is and ought to be totally dissolved; and that as FREE AND INDEPENDENT STATES; they have full Power to levy War, conclude Peace, contract Alliances, establish Commerce, and to do all other Acts and Things which Independent States may of right do. And for the support of this Declaration, with a firm reliance on the protection of Divine Providence, We mutually pledge to each other our Lives, our Fortunes, and our sacred Honor.

Notes

Introduction: The Man Who Wrote the Declaration

1. Quoted in Roy P. Basler, ed., *Abraham Lincoln: His Speeches and Writings*. Cleveland: World Publishing, 1946, p. 577.
2. Quoted in Sarah N. Randolph, *The Domestic Life of Thomas Jefferson*. Charlottesville: University Press of Virginia, 1978, p. 26.
3. Garry Wills, *Inventing America: Jefferson's Declaration of Independence*. Garden City, NY: Doubleday, 1978, p. 14.
4. Quoted in Wills, *Inventing America*, pp. 14–15.
5. Quoted in Basler, *Abraham Lincoln*, p. 489.

Chapter 1: Britain's Abuses of Its American Colonies

6. Irwin Unger, *These United States. The Questions of Our Past, Volume I*. New York: Prentice-Hall, 2002, p. 58.
7. Unger, *These United States*, p. 47.
8. Samuel E. Morison, *The Oxford History of the American People*. New York: Oxford University Press, 1965, p. 185.
9. Quoted in Thomas Fleming, *Liberty!: The American Revolution*. New York: Viking Penguin, 1997, p. 50.
10. Quoted in Fleming, *Liberty!*, p. 51.
11. Morison, *Oxford History of the American People*, p. 186.
12. Unger, *These United States*, p. 111.
13. John Adams, *Diary and Autobiography*, ed. L. H. Butterfield et al. 4 vols. Cambridge: Harvard University Press, 1961, vol. 2, p. 102.
14. Quoted in Fleming, *Liberty!*, p. 86.
15. Quoted in Henry S. Commager and Richard B. Morris, eds., *The Spirit of 'Seventy-Six: The Story of the American Revolution as Told by Participants*. 2 vols. New York: Bobbs-Merrill, 1958, vol. 1, p. 39.
16. Quoted in Richard Hofstadter et al., *The United States: The History of a Republic*. Englewood Cliffs, NJ: Prentice-Hall, 1957, p. 98.
17. Thomas Jefferson, *A Summary View of the Rights of British America*, in Merrill D. Peterson, ed., *Thomas Jefferson: Writings*. New York: Library of America, 1984, p. 118.
18. Jefferson, *Summary View*, in Peterson, *Thomas Jefferson: Writings*, p. 121.

Chapter 2: The Decision to Declare Independence

19. Quoted in Alden T. Vaughan, ed., *Chronicles of the Revolution*. New York: Grosset and Dunlap, 1965, p. 235.
20. Quoted in Morison, *Oxford History of the American People*, pp. 213–14.
21. Quoted in Fleming, *Liberty!*, pp. 112–13.
22. Thomas Paine, *Common Sense*, in John Dos Passos, *John Dos Passos Presents the Living Thoughts of Tom Paine*. New York: Fawcett, 1963, pp. 60, 78.
23. Quoted in Morison, *Oxford History of the American People*, p. 216.
24. Quoted in Commager and Morris, *Spirit of 'Seventy-Six*, vol. 1, p. 281.
25. Quoted in Dos Passos, *Living Thoughts of Tom Paine*, pp. 64–66.
26. Quoted in Commager and Morris, *Spirit of 'Seventy-Six*, vol. 1, p. 295.
27. Quoted in Commager and Morris, *Spirit of 'Seventy-Six*, vol. 1, p. 302.
28. Quoted in Adrienne Koch and William Peden, eds., *The Life and Selected Writings of Thomas Jefferson*. New York: Random House, 1944, pp. 19–20.
29. Joseph J. Ellis, *American Sphinx: The Character of Thomas Jefferson*. New York: Knopf, 1997, p. 49.

30. Quoted in Peterson, *Thomas Jefferson: Writings*, p. 15.

Chapter 3: Jefferson Writes the Declaration

31. Peterson, *Thomas Jefferson: Writings*, p. 90.
32. Quoted in Commager and Morris, *Spirit of 'Seventy-Six*, vol. 1, p. 315.
33. For this and the following passages from Jefferson's rough draft, see Carl Becker, *The Declaration of Independence: A Study in the History of Political Ideas*. New York: Harcourt Brace, 1922, pp. 141–51.
34. Aristotle, *Ethics*, published as *The Ethics of Aristotle*, trans. J.A.K. Thomson, rev. Hugh Tredennick. New York: Penguin, 1976, pp. 189–90.
35. Cicero, *The Republic*, in *Cicero: The Republic and the Laws*, trans. Niall Rudd. New York: Oxford University Press, 1998, pp. 68–69.
36. John Locke, *The Second Treatise of Government*, ed. Thomas P. Peardon. Indianapolis: Bobbs-Merrill, 1952, pp. 4–6.
37. Locke, *Second Treatise*, p. 128.
38. Quoted in Diane Ravitch and Abigail Thernstrom, eds., *The Democracy Reader*. New York: HarperCollins, 1992, p. 41.
39. Quoted in Koch and Peden, *Life and Selected Writings of Thomas Jefferson*, p. 22.
40. Thomas Jefferson, Preamble to Virginia Constitution, in Edward Dumbauld, *The Declaration of Independence and What It Means Today*. Norman: University of Oklahoma Press, 1950, pp. 162–63.
41. From the final version of the Declaration of Independence, in Koch and Peden, *Life and Selected Writings of Thomas Jefferson*, pp. 23–25.
42. George Mason, *Virginia Bill of Rights*, in Dumbauld, *Declaration of Independence*, p. 168.
43. From the rough draft of the Declaration of Independence, quoted in Becker, *Declaration of Independence*, p. 142.
44. Quoted in Peterson, *Thomas Jefferson: Writings*, p. 1501.

45. Quoted in Dumbauld, *Declaration of Independence*, pp. 168–69.
46. Quoted in Koch and Peden, *Life and Selected Writings of Thomas Jefferson*, p. 23.
47. Ellis, *American Sphinx*, p. 57.
48. Quoted in Dumbauld, *Declaration of Independence*, p. 169.
49. Thomas Paine, *The Rights of Man*, in Dos Passos, *Living Thoughts of Tom Paine*, p. 110.
50. Quoted in Koch and Peden, *Life and Selected Writings of Thomas Jefferson*, p. 23.

Chapter 4: Revising and Ratifying the Declaration

51. Quoted in Commager and Morris, *Spirit of 'Seventy-Six*, vol. 1, p. 314.
52. This and the other initial revisions by the committee cited here appear in Becker, *Declaration of Independence*, pp. 153–56.
53. See Koch and Peden, *Life and Selected Writings of Thomas Jefferson*, pp. 22–23.
54. See Koch and Peden, *Life and Selected Writings of Thomas Jefferson*, pp. 22–23.
55. See Koch and Peden, *Life and Selected Writings of Thomas Jefferson*, pp. 22–23.
56. See Koch and Peden, *Life and Selected Writings of Thomas Jefferson*, pp. 24–25.
57. See Koch and Peden, *Life and Selected Writings of Thomas Jefferson*, pp. 26–27.
58. See Koch and Peden, *Life and Selected Writings of Thomas Jefferson*, pp. 26–27.
59. Quoted in Koch and Peden, *Life and Selected Writings of Thomas Jefferson*, p. 21.
60. Quoted in Ravitch and Thernstrom, *Democracy Reader*, pp. 107–8.
61. Quoted in Becker, *Declaration of Independence*, pp. 212–13.
62. Quoted in Commager and Morris, *Spirit of 'Seventy-Six*, vol. 1, p. 314.
63. Quoted in Commager and Morris, *Spirit of 'Seventy-Six*, vol. 1, p. 315.
64. Ellis, *American Sphinx*, p. 60.
65. Quoted in Commager and Morris, *Spirit of 'Seventy-Six*, vol. 1, p. 315.
66. Quoted in Commager and Morris, *Spirit of*

'Seventy-Six, vol. 1, p. 315.

67. Quoted in Commager and Morris, *Spirit of 'Seventy-Six*, vol. 1, p. 315.
68. Merrill D. Peterson, *Thomas Jefferson and the New Nation*. New York: Oxford University Press, 1970, p. 92.
69. Fleming, *Liberty!*, p. 176.

Chapter 5: The War to Enforce the Declaration

70. Quoted in Commager and Morris, *Spirit of 'Seventy-Six*, vol. 1, pp. 322–23.
71. Quoted in Commager and Morris, *Spirit of 'Seventy-Six*, vol. 1, p. 62.
72. Charles Inglis, *The True Interest of America Impartially Stated, in Certain Strictures on a Pamphlet Intitled Common Sense*, quoted in William Dudley, ed., *The American Revolution: Opposing Viewpoints*. San Diego: Greenhaven Press, 1992, pp. 154–55.
73. Hofstadter, *The United States*, p. 105.
74. Quoted in Morison, *Oxford History of the American People*, p. 243.
75. Fleming, *Liberty!*, p. 216.
76. Fleming, *Liberty!*, p. 215.
77. Morison, *Oxford History of the American People*, pp. 243–44.
78. Quoted in Commager and Morris, *Spirit of 'Seventy-Six*, vol. 1, pp. 577–78.
79. Quoted in Commager and Morris, *Spirit of 'Seventy-Six*, vol. 2, pp. 919–20.
80. Quoted in Commager and Morris, *Spirit of 'Seventy-Six*, vol. 1, p. 220.
81. Quoted in Fleming, *Liberty!*, p. 312.
82. Quoted in Morison, *Oxford History of the American People*, p. 263.
83. Morison, *Oxford History of the American People*, p. 265.

Chapter 6: The Declaration Inspires a Larger Revolution

84. Dumas Malone, *Jefferson the Virginian*. Boston: Little Brown, 1948, p. 223.
85. Quoted in Lally Weymouth, ed., *Thomas Jefferson: The Man, His World, His Influence*. London: Weidenfeld and Nicolson, 1973, p. 183.
86. Quoted in Peterson, *Thomas Jefferson: Writings*, p. 1517.
87. Quoted in Koch and Peden, *Life and Selected Writings of Thomas Jefferson*, p. 72.
88. Quoted in Simon Schama, *Citizens: A Chronicle of the French Revolution*. New York: Knopf, 1989, p. 49.
89. Quoted in Koch and Peden, *Life and Selected Writings of Thomas Jefferson*, p. 72.
90. Quoted in Schama, *Citizens*, p. 48.
91. Quoted in Schama, *Citizens*, p. 48.
92. J.L. Talmon, *Romanticism and Revolt: Europe 1815–1848*. New York: Harcourt Brace and World, 1967, p. 51.
93. Melvin Kranzberg, ed., *1848: A Turning Point?* Boston: D.C. Heath, 1959, p. xi.
94. James F. Hoge Jr. and Fareed Zakaria, eds., *The American Encounter: The United States and the Making of the Modern World*. New York: BasicBooks, 1997, p. 9.
95. Quoted in Hoge and Zakaria, *American Encounter*, p. 3.
96. Quoted in Ravitch and Thernstrom, *Democracy Reader*, pp. 202–3.
97. Quoted in Ravitch and Thernstrom, *Democracy Reader*, p. 203.
98. Quoted in Ravitch and Thernstrom, *Democracy Reader*, p. 204.
99. J. Franklin Jameson, *The American Revolution Considered as a Social Movement*. Princeton: Princeton University Press, 1926, p. 9.
100. Quoted in Basler, *Abraham Lincoln*, p. 577.

For Further Reading

Books

Herbert M. Atherton and J. Jackson Barlow, eds., *1791–1991, The Bill of Rights and Beyond*. Washington, DC: Commission on the Bicentennial of the United States Constitution, 1990. This very handsomely mounted book, which is available in most schools and libraries, features many stunning photos and drawings that perfectly highlight the readable text summarizing the impact of the original ten amendments to the Constitution.

Richard Ferrie, *The World Turned Upside Down: George Washington and the Battle of Yorktown*. New York: Holiday House Books, 1999. A lavishly illustrated and very well-written description of the victory that decided the Revolutionary War. Highly recommended for young readers.

Kathy Furgang, *The Declaration of Independence and John Adams of Massachusetts*. New York: Powerkids Press, 2002. Covers Adams's role in the events of 1776, including his work on the drafting committee of the Declaration.

———, *The Declaration of Independence and Richard Henry Lee of Virginia*. New York: Powerkids Press, 2002. Another of Ms. Furgang's volumes about the creation of the United States, this one focuses on Lee, whose resolution made the colonies' split with Britain official.

Don Nardo, *Opposing Viewpoints Digests: The Bill of Rights*. San Diego: Greenhaven Press, 1997; and *Opposing Viewpoints Digests: The Revolutionary War*, San Diego: Greenhaven Press, 1998. These volumes provide a collection of extensively documented essays containing a wide range of opinions and debates about the American war for independence, rights, equality, and the important figures involved.

———, *Thomas Jefferson*. New York: Franklin Watts, 2003. This biography of Jefferson, aimed at junior high school readers, includes his role as principal author of the Declaration of Independence as well as his other contributions to the formation of the early United States.

Dian Silox-Jarrett, *Heroines of the American Revolution: America's Founding Mothers*. Chapel Hill, NC: Green Angel Press, 1998. Has a lot of interesting information for young readers about some of the women who played important parts in the Revolutionary War. Be aware that some of the dialogue is fictional.

Gail B. Stewart, *The Revolutionary War*. San Diego: Lucent Books, 1991. One of the best current writers for young adults does a fine job chronicling the main events of the war between Britain and its American colonies.

Websites

The Charters of Freedom, U.S. National Archives and Records Administration (www.archives.gov) This informative site contains links leading to the full texts of major U.S. historical documents, including the Declaration of Independence and Constitution.

Original Rough Draft of the Declaration of Independence, Library of Congress (www. loc.gov) Provides the complete text of Jefferson's original draft for the Declaration, which Congress amended.

Thomas Jefferson, The White House (www. whitehouse.gov) The official White House biography of Jefferson. The site also has links to similar biographies of all the other presidents and other information about the government.

Major Works Consulted

Modern Sources

Carl Becker, *The Declaration of Independence: A Study in the History of Political Ideas*. New York: Harcourt Brace, 1922. A well-written and useful book, thought by many historians to be the most insightful modern volume written about the Declaration.

Julian P. Boyd, *The Declaration of Independence: The Evolution of the Text as Shown in Facsimiles of Various Drafts by Its Author*. Princeton: Princeton University Press, 1945. This thorough scholarly work is one of the two (the other being Becker's book, above) most often used by historians in analyzing the various drafts of the Declaration.

Gilbert Chinard, *Thomas Jefferson: The Apostle of Americanism*. Ann Arbor: University of Michigan Press, 1966. This scholarly work emphasizes Jefferson's contributions to the formation of American and democratic thought and values.

Edward Countryman, *The American Revolution*. New York: Hill and Wang, 1985. Arguably the most authoritative single-volume general history of the American war for independence, this is a large, richly documented, and engrossing study. Highly recommended.

Thomas Fleming, *Liberty!: The American Revolution*. New York: Viking Penguin, 1997. A superb telling of the American war for independence, including a great deal on the events leading up to it. Contains numerous primary source quotations, many of them rarely seen in other texts.

Eric Foner, *Tom Paine and Revolutionary America*. New York: Oxford University Press, 1976. This biography of the fiery Revolutionary who penned the widely influential *Common Sense* effectively covers the social and political panorama of the American colonies of his era. Well written, superbly documented, and generally superior of its kind.

Gary Hart, *Restoration of the Republic: The Jeffersonian Ideal in 21st-Century America*. New York: Oxford University Press, 2002. A compelling examination of the republican ideals Jefferson infused into the Declaration of Independence and his other writings and how those ideals find voice today.

Merrill Jensen, *The Founding of a Nation: A History of the American Revolution, 1763–1776*. New York: Oxford University Press, 1968. Jensen, one of the major historians of the Revolutionary period, here explores the writings, speeches, actions, and reactions of the colonists in the formative years of the founding of the United States.

Dumas Malone, *Jefferson the Virginian*. Boston: Little, Brown, 1948. This first volume of Malone's epic, prodigiously researched and documented, and masterfully written six-volume study, is widely acclaimed as the most authoritative multivolume biography of Jefferson; it contains much valuable information about Jefferson's early political activities and his drafting of the Declaration of Independence.

Edmund S. Morgan and Helen M. Morgan, *The Stamp Act Crisis: Prologue to Revolution*. Chapel Hill, NC: University of North Carolina Press, 1953. A highly detailed and comprehensive scholarly study of the background of the Stamp Act, British motivations for implementing it, America's irate reactions to it, the act's repeal, and how the crisis foreshadowed the coming struggle between the colonies and the mother country.

Merrill D. Peterson, *Thomas Jefferson and the New Nation*. New York: Oxford University Press, 1970. The best and most authoritative existing single-volume biography of Jefferson, Peterson's work contains a great deal of information about the genesis and completion of the Declaration of Independence. Very highly recommended.

Hugh F. Rankin, *The American Revolution*. New York: G.P. Putnam's Sons, 1964. Rankin, formerly of Tulane University, here effectively covers the highlights of the U.S. war for independence through a chain of long, colorful, and often dramatic eyewitness accounts from the period (each preceded by an informative preface by the author).

Carl J. Richard, *The Founders and the Classics*. Cambridge: Harvard University Press, 1994. A scholarly study of the influence of ancient Greco-Roman political ideals on the democratic thought of Thomas Jefferson and the other U.S. founders.

Clinton Rossiter, *Seedtime of the Republic: The Origin of the American Tradition of Political Liberty*. New York: Harcourt Brace and World, 1953. The widely respected former Cornell University scholar won a number of literary awards for this study, an original one for its time, which examines the political ideas that shaped the American Revolution and how those ideas became part of the fabric of the documents and institutions of the infant United States. Will be of interest mainly to scholars and teachers.

Harry M. Ward, *The American Revolution: Nationhood Achieved, 1763–1788*. New York:
St. Martin's Press, 1995. A fine, up-to-date, quite detailed overview of the American march toward independence, the struggle with Britain, and the early formative years of the new American nation.

Lally Weymouth, ed., *Thomas Jefferson: The Man, His World, His Influence*. London: Weidenfeld and Nicolson, 1973. An excellent collection of essays about Jefferson, each by a world-class historian. Of special interest here are "Jefferson and the Enlightenment," by Henry Steele Commager; "Prolegomena to a Reading of the Declaration," by Garry Wills; and "The Declaration of Independence," also by Commager.

Garry Wills, *Inventing America: Jefferson's Declaration of Independence*. Garden City, NY: Doubleday, 1978. A detailed study of the Declaration that makes the case that the deleted sections of Jefferson's original draft contain much of the true meaning of the document.

Primary Sources

The following volumes (or sets of volumes) are comprehensive and invaluable mines of primary sources materials, each containing from several dozen to more than a hundred complete or partial documents (letters, pamphlets, newspaper articles, journals, town records, and so on) from the formative era of the United States.

Bernard Bailyn, ed., *Pamphlets of the American Revolution*. Cambridge: Harvard University Press, 1965.

Max Beloff, ed., *The Debate on the American Revolution, 1761–1783*. London: Adam and Charles Black, 1960.

Henry S. Commager and Richard B. Morris, eds., *The Spirit of 'Seventy-Six: The Story of the American Revolution as Told by Participants*. 2 vols. New York: Bobbs-Merrill, 1958.

Catherine S. Crary, ed., *The Price of Loyalty: Tory Writings from the Revolutionary Era.* New York: McGraw-Hill, 1973.

John C. Dann, ed., *The Revolution Remembered: Eyewitness Accounts of the War for Independence.* Chicago: University of Chicago Press, 1980.

William Dudley, ed., *The American Revolution: Opposing Viewpoints.* San Diego: Greenhaven Press, 1992.

Carl J. Friedrich and Robert G. McCloskey, eds., *From the Declaration of Independence to the Constitution: The Roots of American Constitutionalism.* Indianapolis: Bobbs-Merrill, 1954.

Samuel E. Morison, ed., *Sources and Documents Illustrating the American Revolution, 1764–1788, and the Formation of the Federal Constitution.* Oxford, England: Clarendon Press, 1953.

Richard B. Morris, ed., *The American Revolution, 1763–1783: A Bicentennial Collection.* Columbia: University of South Carolina Press, 1970.

Diane Ravitch, ed., *The American Reader: Words That Moved a Nation.* New York: HarperCollins, 1990.

Diane Ravitch and Abigail Thernstrom, eds., *The Democracy Reader.* New York: HarperCollins, 1992.

Alden T. Vaughan, ed., *Chronicles of the Revolution.* New York: Grosset and Dunlap, 1965.

Other Primary Sources

John Adams, *Diary and Autobiography.* Ed. L.H. Butterfield et al. 4 vols. Cambridge: Harvard University Press, 1961.

Aristotle, *Ethics*, published as *The Ethics of Aristotle.* Trans. J.A.K. Thomson, rev. Hugh Tredennick. New York: Penguin, 1976.

Roy P. Basler, ed., *Abraham Lincoln: His Speeches and Writings.* Cleveland: World Publishing, 1946.

Isaiah Berlin, ed., *The Age of Enlightenment: The 18th Century Philosophers.* New York: New American Library, 1956.

Cicero, *The Republic*, in *Cicero: The Republic and the Laws.* Trans. Niall Rudd. New York: Oxford University Press, 1998.

John Dos Passos, *John Dos Passos Presents the Living Thoughts of Tom Paine.* New York: Fawcett, 1963.

Adrienne Koch and William Peden, eds., *The Life and Selected Writings of Thomas Jefferson.* New York: Random House, 1944.

A.A. Lipscomb and A.E. Bergh, eds., *The Writings of Thomas Jefferson.* 20 vols. Washington, DC: Thomas Jefferson Memorial Association of the United States, 1903.

John Locke, *The Second Treatise of Government.* Ed. Thomas P. Peardon. Indianapolis: Bobbs-Merrill, 1952.

Merrill D. Peterson, ed., *Thomas Jefferson: Writings.* New York: Library of America, 1984.

Sarah N. Randolph, *The Domestic Life of Thomas Jefferson.* Charlottesville: University Press of Virginia, 1978.

James Thatcher, *A Military Journal During the American Revolutionary War, from 1775–1783, Describing Interesting Events and Transactions of This Period.* Boston: Cottons and Barnard, 1827.

Additional Works Consulted

David Ammerman, *In Common Cause: American Response to the Coercive Acts of 1774.* Charlottesville: University Press of Virginia, 1974.

George A. Billias, ed., *The American Revolution: How Revolutionary Was It?* New York: Holt, Rinehart, and Winston, 1965.

Stewart G. Brown, *Thomas Jefferson.* New York: Washington Square Press, 1963.

Philip Davidson, *Propaganda and the American Revolution, 1763–1783.* New York: W.W. Norton, 1973.

Edward Dumbauld, *The Declaration of Independence and What It Means Today.* Norman: University of Oklahoma Press, 1950.

Joseph J. Ellis, *American Sphinx: The Character of Thomas Jefferson.* New York: Knopf, 1997.

———, *Founding Brothers: The Revolutionary Generation.* New York: Vintage, 2002.

Thomas Fleming, *1776: Year of Illusion.* New York: W.W. Norton, 1975.

Thomas Flexner, *George Washington.* Boston: Little, Brown, 1968.

Richard Hofstadter et al., *The United States: The History of a Republic.* Englewood Cliffs, NJ: Prentice-Hall, 1957.

James F. Hoge Jr. and Fareed Zakaria, eds., *The American Encounter: The United States and the Making of the Modern World.* New York: BasicBooks, 1997.

J. Franklin Jameson, *The American Revolution Considered as a Social Movement.* Princeton: Princeton University Press, 1926.

Merrill Jenson, *The Making of the American Constitution.* New York: D. Van Nostrand, 1964.

Melvin Kranzberg, ed., *1848: A Turning Point?* Boston: D.C. Heath, 1959.

Earl Latham, ed., *The Declaration of Independence and the Constitution.* Boston: D.C. Heath, 1956.

Piers Mackesy, *The War for America, 1775–1783.* Cambridge: Harvard University Press, 1964.

Pauline Maier, *From Resistance to Revolution.* New York: Knopf, 1972.

Edward G. McGrath, *Is American Democracy Exportable?* Beverly Hills: Glencoe Press, 1968.

Samuel E. Morison, *The Oxford History of the American People.* New York: Oxford University Press, 1965.

Henry A. Myers, *Are Men Equal? An Inquiry into the Meaning of American Democracy.* Ithaca: Cornell University Press, 1963.

Simon Schama, *Citizens: A Chronicle of the French Revolution.* New York: Knopf, 1989.

J.L. Talmon, *Romanticism and Revolt: Europe 1815–1848.* New York: Harcourt Brace and World, 1967.

Irwin Unger, *These United States. The Questions of Our Past, Volume I.* New York: Prentice-Hall, 2002.

John C. Wahlke, ed., *The Causes of the American Revolution.* Boston: D.C. Heath, 1950.

Francis G. Walett, *Patriots, Loyalists, and Printers: Bicentennial Articles on the American*

Revolution. Worcester, MA: American Antiquarian Society, 1976.

Gordon S. Wood, *The Radicalism of the American Revolution.* New York: Knopf, 1992.

Fareed Zakaria, "The Rise of Illiberal Democracy," *Foreign Affairs,* November 1997.

Howard Zinn, *A People's History of the United States.* New York: HarperCollins, 1980.

Index

British military
    arrogance of, 68, 70
    defeats of, 68–70, 74–75
    superior strength of, 65–68
    surrender by, 75–76
British navy, 66, 70–72
British troops, 26
Brooklyn Heights, Battle of, 67
Bunker Hill, Battle of, 33
Burgoyne, George, 9
Burgoyne, John, 70

capitalism, 87
Central America, 86
Cicero, 43–44
civil rights, 91
class distinctions, 82–83
Coercive Acts. *See* Intolerable Acts
Collins, James, 73
Commager, Henry S., 38, 77
Common Sense (Paine), 9, 34–35
Concord, Battle of, 32
Condorcet, Marquis de, 82
Connecticut, 14
Continental army
    initial losses suffered by, 67–68
    small size of, 66
    victories by, 68–70, 74–75
Continental Congress, 8
    adoption of Suffolk Resolves by, 27
    delegates to, 24–25
    peacekeeping attempts by, 32–34
    resolution on independence by, 35–36, 53
Continental navy, 66, 70–72
Cornwallis, Lord Charles, 9, 73, 74–75
Cowpens, Battle of, 74

Declaration of Independence
    antislavery passage in original, 56–59
    debate over, in Congress, 53, 55–59
    form of argument in, 40–42
    inspiring phrases in, 52
    Jefferson asked to draft, 36–38

lasting inspiration of, 77–91
list of grievances in, 47, 48
melting pot of ideas in, 48–50
original copy of, 80
public reaction to, 64–65
revisions made to, 51–59
revolutions inspired by, 81–87
signing of, 9, 61–63
sources for, 39–40, 42–50
spread of democracy and, 77–80
text of, 92–95
writing of, by Jefferson, 9, 39–50
Declaration on the Rights of Man and
    Citizen, 83–84
democracy
    liberal, 88
    spread of, 77–80, 84–87
d'Estaing, Comte, 72
Dickinson, John, 22, 33
Drake (ship), 72
Duché, Jacob, 67

Ellis, Joseph J., 36–37, 59
emigration, 81
English settlers, 14–16
Enlightenment thought, 39, 42–44
Europe, revolutions in, 85

Farmer's Letters (Dickinson), 22
Fars-Fausselandry, Vicomtesse de, 81–82
First Continental Congress. *See* Continental
    Congress
Fleming, Thomas, 61, 68
Founders and the Classics, The (Richard), 43
France
    American alliance with, 35, 72, 74
    former power of, 87
    role of, in peace treaty signing, 75–76
Franklin, Benjamin
    on Declaration committee, 36
    influence of, on Declaration, 47
    revisions made to Declaration by, 51–52
    at signing of Declaration, 62

Picture Credits

About the Author

Historian and award-winning author Don Nardo has written many books for young people about American history, including *The Bill of Rights, The War of 1812, The Mexican-American War, The Great Depression, Pearl Harbor*, and biographies of Thomas Jefferson, Andrew Johnson, and Franklin D. Roosevelt. Mr. Nardo lives with his wife, Christine, in Massachusetts.

DATE			